Fitness over 50, 60, 70 and Beyond

Dr. Michael Guadagnino, III, BS, DC

ISBN: 979-8-89122-420-9

Dedication

This book is dedicated to Generation X, the only generation that became 30 at the age of 10 and is still 30 at the age of 50.

By taking care of our health and wellness, we will remain forever 30!

Acknowledgment

Thank you to the countless doctors, fitness trainers, nutritionists and alternative healthcare providers that dedicate their lives to keeping the public healthy....naturally. Behind the loud white noise is an abundance of knowledge that can extend human longevity.

Thank you to my wife Jennifer, and adult children Michael IV & Nicole. The examples I set have always been influenced by my ever-present awareness of your watchful gaze. Each of you are very successful in your own right, and are forever an inspiration to me.

Table of Contents

About the Author

Dr. Michael Guadagnino, III, has been a practicing Chiropractic Physician since 1991, a recreation commissioner for twenty years, a black belt in karate since the age of twelve, holds a Bachelor of Science in Biology and is a fitness guru for those over the age of 50. He has been a featured guest on News 12, New Jersey, and has been published in scientific journals.

Throughout his youth and continuing into adulthood, Dr. Guadagnino has incorporated exercise, diet, positive thinking, social engagement, and the many elements essential for a healthy lifestyle into his everyday life. He serves as a role model for healthy living, and his patients and followers appreciate the authenticity of his message.

Dr. Guadagnino's passion stems from observing a significant portion of the population over the age of 50, relying on medication for chronic illness, struggling with maintaining a healthy weight or living with physical limitations due to lack of strength and flexibility. Many of these individuals need motivation and knowledge to enable them to take an active role in improving their health, fitness, and overall quality of life.

He is highly optimistic in his message and confident that readers of this book will be encouraged and supported to achieve higher levels of wellness through organized strategies that inspire and guide. Dr. Guadagnino is committed to making a difference, believing he can help change the world by keeping the aging community healthier and more active for many years to come!

Page Left Blank Intentionally

Introduction

Staying fit into your middle age and senior years is about avoiding toxins, poisons, and anything detrimental to your physical, mental, and emotional well-being. Choosing to be fit over 50, 60, 70, and beyond puts us in a unique category. Look around you: how many people, in their middle and later years, can you say are fit and healthy?

This book speaks to the person who resists taking that long, quiet stroll as their life comes close to an end. We intend to show those who still want their light to shine how to become and stay healthy while resisting the conventional wisdom of aging. Fitness is not about squeaking out a couple of extra years while clinging to a life of illness and misery. Fitness is about having a clear mind, clear arteries, and a clear path to staying healthy. You can achieve the proverbial outcome of "adding years to your life and life to your years," which can be reached with simple lifestyle changes and a commitment to your new regimen. This book is not a difficult read; go through it with a highlighter, pen, or pencil in hand to jot down important points that resonate with you and help you reach your health and fitness goals.

You may choose to have your wrinkles injected, your hair dyed, or to use any products to look younger. Those are all temporary outward changes, but this book is not about that. I want you to be fit—very fit and healthy. Cosmetic changes are your choice, but they won't change what's going on inside your body. Botox won't help you live longer or healthier. Fitness is something you need to work on actively. People are free to do whatever they wish cosmetically, but the intent of this book is to guide you toward becoming healthy and fit. Cosmetic choices will not make you healthy and fit.

The small decisions you make today can profoundly affect where your life may be in five days, five months, or five years. Fitness is about making choices that put you on a path of wellness so you can thrive as you age. You can be that spry elderly person who throws a ball with their grandchild, does not rely on a plethora of daily medications, and genuinely lives a clean, healthy life. The sooner you make changes that impact your health and fitness, the brighter your future will be. Those over the age of 50 still have a bright future. Take control of your health today so you can live spry and strong as you mature. Follow the strategies and lessons in this book if you want your future self to be grateful for the choices you make today.

Some striking examples that illustrate my point are Joan Campbell, Jack LaLanne, and Chuck Norris. The least well-known of these three is Joan Campbell. At age 59, Joan took up competitive swimming. She transformed her life in middle age by working out regularly, including aerobics, swimming, and yoga. She focused on long-term goals, and in her late 80s, she boasted about keeping up with her great-grandchildren. At 92 years old, Joan finished a 1500-meter swimming race in 50:14. Joan is an inspiration to those who aspire to health, wellness, and fitness regardless of age. She made a commitment to maintain her youthful spirit and not allow her health to fade away. She demonstrates that anyone dedicated to improving their well-being can defy the process of aging.

Jack LaLanne lived for 96 years and only became ill the week before his passing. Many would agree that longevity with health is aspirational. He was spry, active, and enjoyed life. Early in his life, Jack considered himself a sugar addict and lived on junk food. He also had a rambunctious side that often got him into trouble. At the age of 15, Jack made a conscious effort to improve his life. He began by altering his diet and eating only clean, non-chemically modified foods. As he made this change, many of his destructive adolescent behaviors also changed. This transformation led him to become a health and fitness guru to millions. At 70 years old, while handcuffed and shackled, Jack pulled 70 boats tied together, each carrying one person for a mile and a half through the Long Beach Harbor. Jack inspired many and used his life to help others live a more fit existence.

Another famous octogenarian who lives a fit life is Chuck Norris. As I write this, he is 84 years young. He has participated in martial arts and fitness for almost his entire life. As a child, Chuck was an extreme introvert. After serving in the military, he began participating in martial arts tournaments, though initially, he did not win many competitive karate bouts. Chuck did not give up and eventually began winning regularly, becoming a karate juggernaut. Chuck has used diet and exercise his entire life to stay healthy and fit. Today, at 84, he still exercises regularly and acts in movies. For his 84th birthday, he participated in a video showing him punching a heavy bag. He turned to the camera and said, "You know I'm 84 today, but I feel like I'm 48."

A U.S. Department of Health and Human Services study estimated that over 41.9% of Americans are overweight. [1]It

---

[1] Stierman, B., Afful, J., Carroll, M., Chen, T.-C., Davy, O., Fink, S., Fryar, C., Gu, Q., Hales, C., Hughes, J., Yechiam Ostchega, M., Renee, R., Storandt, J., & Akinbami, L. (2021). National Health and Nutrition Examination Survey 2017-March 2020 Prepandemic Data Files-Development of Files and Prevalence Estimates for Selected Health Outcomes. National Health Statistics Reports Number, 158(158) https://www.cdc.gov/nchs/data/nhsr/nhsr158-508.pdf

is also known that obesity causes heart disease, stroke, and early death. Another detriment of being overweight includes the medications that many people suffering from obesity take daily to maintain normal body homeostasis. Not to be ignored is the stress obesity puts on joints, ligaments, and cartilage, which makes it difficult for people to walk, bend, and live pain-free lives.

Another study, this one by the Centers for Disease Control and Prevention, estimates that 34 million Americans live with Type II diabetes. [2]Type II diabetes is directly linked to a poor diet and a sedentary lifestyle. Unfortunately, it is a common occurrence among those who are overweight. If left unchecked, diabetes can cause hardening of the arteries, vision issues, heart and kidney problems, and extremity pain, to name just a few symptoms. A person with Type II diabetes may experience an accelerated aging process.

In addition to Type II diabetes, adults who were obese had far worse outcomes during the COVID-19 pandemic. Thirty percent of those hospitalized were obese. Other comorbidities, such as diabetes, heart disease, and

---

[2] CDC. (2024, May 15). *About Type 2 Diabetes*. Diabetes. https://www.cdc.gov/diabetes/about/about-type-2-diabetes.html

atherosclerosis, increase the risk of hospitalization and death.

In February 2024, the Journal of the American Medical Association released a paper on this exact correlation, stating: "In this cohort study, sufficiently active participants had significantly reduced odds of SARS-CoV-2 infection and of hospitalization due to COVID-19 compared with those who were inactive." [3]The mean age for these participants was 75.7 years old. This research paper compared those who were fit to those who were not and how their immune systems responded during the COVID-19 pandemic. Fitness over 50 is not only about looking and feeling good; it's about having your organs, systems, and entire body working as they did when you were young. Giving in to age or the aging process does not benefit you, nor does it help those who want you around for a long time.

Many health conditions can be prevented or eased by a fit lifestyle. Health and wellness can add years to your life, regardless of whether you are over 50, 60, 70, or older. It is never too late, and no one is ever too old to start. This

---

[3] Muñoz-Vergara, D., Wayne, P. M., Kim, E., Lee, I-Min., Buring, J. E., Manson, J. E., & Sesso, H. D. (2024). Prepandemic Physical Activity and Risk of COVID-19 Diagnosis and Hospitalization in Older Adults. JAMA Network Open, 7(2), e2355808–e2355808. https://doi.org/10.1001/jamanetworkopen.2023.55808

includes movement as well as everything you ingest—food, supplements, and liquids.

Looking at today's food industry, it is inundated with processed, artificial, and chemically derived products—what we call food. Many include ingredients that are harmful to your overall health. It is essential to always look at the labels and see what ingredients are included. Investigate what you are putting into your body. An important rule is that the fewer ingredients—especially those not easily recognized—the better. Even with fewer ingredients, know what those ingredients are. This book will include a chapter on the various types of diets. Not every diet or style of eating is suitable for everyone. Each of us has a different body chemistry and a different set of food ethics. Some people are opposed to eating any animal products, while others follow strict religious food traditions. There is diversity in food options, all of which can keep you healthy—or, if consumed without a conscious effort toward healthy living, can lead you down a path of illness and disease. Do not trust the food industry; always read the packaging and take control of your diet.

Every fit person engages in some type of regular exercise. Everyone's "regular" is different; some may do yoga, some may lift weights, others may do calisthenics, etc.

If you're just starting a workout regimen, you will need to pace yourself and work at a slower rate. Don't compare yourself to someone who has worked out for years. The important thing is to work out at your own pace and push yourself safely. Trying to match someone else's workout routine is a recipe for disaster; be yourself.

Over the years, I have treated many patients who were injured by overdoing their workouts. Nothing is wrong with pushing your limits and expanding your endurance and strength. Getting stronger requires exerting your muscles and asking them to lift more weight. The problem for many is that when they push themselves too hard, they can use improper mechanics and fatigue their muscles, joints, and ligaments, which leads to injuries. Shin splints, pulled muscles, herniated discs, and other injuries can be caused by skipping steps in your workout rather than progressing when you are ready. You need to go from A to B to C; you cannot skip from A to B to G. I will discuss the importance of strengthening corresponding muscles to help prevent many injuries. For example, strong triceps will help you bench press more effectively while taking pressure off your shoulders. I will emphasize the importance of proper mechanics throughout this book.

As we go through this journey, we will cover a wide range of topics, from the physical to the mental. This book is for anyone over the age of 50—whether you're turning 50 soon or are in your 80s. Some topics may seem more appropriate for one age group or another, while some information may seem perfectly suited for you. Anyone over 50 can learn about health as they begin to make positive changes toward becoming fit. Don't skip over anything; there is always something new to learn. Remember, aging is a gift. In 1800, life expectancy was only 35 years old. Let's grow old together, with flexibility, strength, a sharp mind, and overall good health.

Chapter One: Good Thoughts, Good Words, Good Deeds — Zarathustra

Aging is natural; embrace the wisdom, experience, and knowledge gained with every year. How you handle maturing will make all the difference in the world. Are you going to fight the degenerative process, or are you going to throw your hands up and surrender? We all get older—our joints ache, our faces wrinkle, and if we stay up late, we feel it the next day. Let us focus on fighting the so-called inevitable by not allowing the clock to win. Like any young athlete who grinds to improve, becoming fit at a later age is a similar grind. On those low-energy days, when heading to the gym seems impossible, stay positive and focused on your long-term goals, and celebrate those small triumphs along the way.

Everything and everyone you come in contact with will have a direct effect on your thoughts, self-identity, and ego. You will manifest everything you see, hear, think, and absorb from all your associations. I start this book with this chapter because the right mindset is needed to begin and maintain a positive and joyful fitness journey. Your thoughts and focus need to be on positivity, no matter your situation. If you have had surgeries, suffer from chronic illness, or have other health issues, you can still be fit. Limitation of matter is fundamental; you have wrinkles because your collagen and subcutaneous fat are not what they were 30 years ago—that's life. Even with these roadblocks, you can still work to express your full genetic possibilities and reach your ultimate health and fitness goals.

I used to work out with a man who had salt-and-pepper hair, named Jim. He had a unique situation: he was confined to a wheelchair. I can still see his black workout gloves, his 1990s-style workout clothes, and his intense determination. Regardless of his situation, Jim would exercise alongside my fellow 20-something-year-old exercise enthusiasts. I was inspired and felt accountable when training with Jim. If Jim could push out that extra rep, then I better do so. I would often spot him during demanding reps; he didn't have to ask. Everyone exercising in the gym would lend him a hand if we saw a need. This is good gym etiquette, which includes helping and supporting one another.

Jim was paralyzed from the waist down. It didn't matter; he would move his wheelchair from one piece of equipment to another. Jim would then position himself on different weight machines and work pretty hard. Most of the time, he didn't need a spot, but like the others in the gym, I was there to encourage him to get that last rep and to assist if he hit a sticking point in his motion. Jim never gave up; he didn't give in to whatever caused him to have this physical challenge. Instead, he continued working on his fitness. At times, he even got tangled in the bottom of different machines and needed someone to move his feet and legs out. This didn't hinder him; he didn't become self-conscious or look for pity. Jim was there for a purpose and was just one of the people we exercised with. He had severe limitations but worked hard to reach his full genetic potential.

Everyone suffers from something, and to each person, it is unique and personal. Jim's debilitation was an extreme version, but he didn't allow it to hold him back. What separates those who find success from those who do not is their response to adversity and how they handle it. Neglecting our health and wellness is never a good idea. Hardships are difficult burdens, but it is important to find that inner strength and path that leads toward reaching our goals.

My experience has taught me that working on small, incremental goals will ultimately lead to achieving bigger goals, including fitness. If you want to lose a specific amount of weight, and you only lose 1 lb. a week or 4 lbs. a month, do not let this get you down. This is a great weight loss path, especially when viewed in the long term. This plan will allow you to lose 50 lbs. in a year and 100 lbs. in two years. Don't get down over what you perceive as failure; fitness is a process.

Similarly, if lifting weights and your physical ability allows you to lift only an empty barbell, that is OK. Over time, slowly add ¼ lbs. when ready. Eventually, you'll add 5 lbs., then 10 lbs., then quarter plates. This is not a race but rather a plan that is always working toward bigger goals. Celebrate the small victories, whether losing 4 lbs. a month or going from a 2½ lbs. plate to a 5 lbs. plate. Fitness is a journey; there is no reason to expect overnight success. Think about anyone you have encountered in your line of work or socially. In my own life, I had to attend undergraduate college as a pre-med student before I could even apply to Chiropractic college. Earning my degree was a 7½-year journey, which included cycles of success and occasional setbacks. If I had gotten frustrated and quit because of challenges in freshman calculus, I would never have earned my degree. Patience, a plan, and follow-through are needed, but your goals can be reached. Focus on consistency in the health and fitness journey rather than speed.

It is also important not to waste energy comparing yourself to others. Fitness is very personal. There are a lot of big talkers in the gym and even bigger talkers online. Don't get caught up in their world; it's a no-win situation. Stay in your world, your biological timeframe, your personal physique, and your goals. The worst thing you can do to yourself is deal with someone else's issues. Remember who you are—you can improve your situation to be fit. Ignore the noise. Knowing who you are and your goals leads to the importance of surrounding yourself with people who are uplifting. Positive people will give you confidence, help you see the good inside of you, and encourage you to work for the greater good within yourself and uplift others. It's a cycle to live by. Your internal thought process will improve; you will think more about "How can I?" instead of "Why can't I?" Hostile thoughts and a hostile life will age you. [1]Rid yourself of toxic people. If you're stuck with these types of people in a workplace or other environment, find a way to not let their words or thoughts affect you. Never allow toxic

---

[1] Brydon, L., Lin, J., Butcher, L., Hamer, M., Erusalimsky, J. D., Blackburn, E. H., & Steptoe, A. (2012). Hostility and Cellular Aging in Men from the Whitehall II Cohort. *Biological Psychiatry*, *71*(9), 767–773. https://doi.org/10.1016/j.biopsych.2011.08.020

people to be a part of your life, and especially do not allow them into your headspace.

No matter how long you may have known someone, if they are not suitable for your mental health, leave them behind. You have no responsibility to anyone who is unhealthy for your mental and physical well-being. They may not even direct their hostility toward you, but being around toxic people will alter your thought process. Similarly, surrounding yourself with positive people will improve your thought process and brain chemistry. Do not mistake a good personality for optimism. Do not mistake false praise or someone simply “telling you what you want to hear” as a positive influence. Listen to people’s words, identify their motivations, and understand the effect they will have on you.

The focus is always to stay away from toxic thoughts. Scientist and Nobel Prize winner Elizabeth Blackburn and psychologist Elissa Epel demonstrated how toxic thoughts can age you. In their book, *The Telomere Effect: A Revolutionary Approach to Living Younger, Healthier, and Longer*, they illustrated that our chromosomes are affected by destructive thoughts. Imagine entering this world and allowing someone else to impact your growth, age, and life negatively. [2]Never allow outside influences to affect you negatively—you deserve better than that!

This takes us back to surrounding yourself with upbeat, positive people. Your thoughts, words, and deeds will manifest around you. Keeping good company will improve your mental, emotional, physical, and spiritual fitness (although belief in the last is an entirely personal matter).

We all know people who suck the wind out of the room. You know who they are—you probably thought of someone when you read that last sentence. These people are not good for your mental well-being. They are exhausting in every aspect. Move on from these types of people; the sad thing is, they probably won't even miss you. Think of your mental health first, and do not worry about disassociating from a toxic individual.

It's important that your internal self-dialogue always speaks in the positive. Believe in yourself, regardless of how many "failures" you may have experienced. Thomas Edison failed thousands of times but instead thought, "I have not

---

[2] *The Telomere Effect: A Revolutionary Approach to Living Younger, Healthier, Longer:* Blackburn, Dr. Elizabeth, Epel, Dr. Elissa: 9781455587971: Amazon.com: Books. (2024). Amazon.com. https://www.amazon.com/Telomere-Effect-Revolutionary-Approach-Healthier/dp/1455587974

failed. I've just found 10,000 ways that won't work." Michael Jordan was cut from his high school basketball team, yet became the greatest basketball player ever. Stephen King had his masterpiece Carrie rejected by publishers 30 times before his book was accepted. Do not give up; do not believe you are somehow less because of past failures. Like Edison, you are learning ways that do not work, and you can now try something new to make it work. Especially do not allow another person's thoughts, prejudices, or toxicity to affect how you think.

Suppose you have tried to diet hundreds of times but still seem to have gained weight; dissect why and work on fixing what doesn't work. If you cannot get traction from exercise, try something else, and again, analyze why. This includes breaking down your exercise form, the amount of weight used, and the number of reps/sets. Keep dissecting until you find what works. The library, the internet, and professionals are out there to help. Do not give up; keep at it and try a different way.

A negative internal dialogue will keep you down, and for what? Try this exercise: Imagine stepping outside yourself and thinking how it would appear if you heard another person speak that same negative dialogue about themselves. With this simple exercise, you might find that elusive positive key to moving past those bad thoughts. One of the things that separates professional athletes from everyone else (besides incredible God-given talent) is their internal dialogue. They always believe they will win, and they always think they will make the shot, block, catch, etc. If you've ever watched a post-game press conference where a reporter asks why something went wrong, the athlete never blinks. They are on a different thought plane. They always believe they can do it, even if it didn't happen that time. We can learn from professional athletes in their approach to overcoming adversity. Success and never giving up is something they embody.

Brett Favre was a three-time NFL Most Valuable Player, two-time NFC Champion, and a Super Bowl Champion. He also threw 336 interceptions, the most ever by a professional football player. He even threw six interceptions in one playoff game, which set a record. If you followed Brett's career, do you think he dwelled on it, let it bother or control him? He returned the following season after those six interceptions and led his team to the playoffs.

Professional athletes believe differently than most; the more successful the athlete, the more they believe in themselves. Several studies have demonstrated the correlation between positive thought and achievement.[3][4]

We can learn from the example professional athletes set with their thought processes. Even if we cannot throw a football 70 yards in the air like Brett, we can still believe in our natural abilities. Negative thoughts will manifest, age you, and stop you from reaching your fitness goals. Keep it positive, learn why something didn't go right, and use it as motivation when—not if—you try again.

Another phrase I always tell my patients, clients, and even my kids is to "Find the joy" in your actions. You may be having a bad day and not like your present life circumstances, but find joy. Your current situation may not be going well, but look for something within it that you can appreciate. If you are in a position that makes it difficult to change, work on small incremental remedies; if you are in danger, leave immediately. Do not remain static: if you do not like something, begin to alter it. Life is hard—no one

---

[3] Shi, Y., & Qu, S. (2022). The effect of cognitive ability on academic achievement: The mediating role of self-discipline and the moderating role of planning. Frontiers in Psychology, 13(13). https://doi.org/10.3389/fpsyg.2022.1014655

[4] Gustafson, C. (2017). Bruce Lipton, PhD: The Jump From Cell Culture to Consciousness. *Integrative Medicine: A Clinician's Journal*, *16*(6), 44. https://pmc.ncbi.nlm.nih.gov/articles/PMC6438088/

ever said it wouldn't be—but becoming fit includes maintaining your mental fitness as you grow older. As noted above, neglecting your health and fitness will not help you. If you are in a situation that requires professional help, seek it out. You only go through this life once, so let's work to improve your situation and live the best life possible.

Fitness is a complete package: body, mind, and psyche. One cannot support the physical without the mental and emotional. Good thoughts will make a difference in your growth. You may be over 50, 60, 70, or beyond, but you should continue growing, learning, and evolving. Muhammad Ali once said, "If you look at the world at 50 the way you did at 20, then you've wasted 30 years." Mental development and growth are ongoing processes that continue until you cease to exist. If you are reading this book and looking to become fit after 50, then you are already seeing the world differently than you did in the past.

A brain that is stagnant or filled with negative thoughts leads to a decaying mind and body, whereas a brain filled with positive thoughts can flourish, grow, and be radiant. If given a choice between darkness and joy, disease and health, or decay and fitness, always choose the latter. You are here to express your fullest potential, and a positive mind gives you the best opportunity to do so. Work hard at keeping your internal thoughts positive—it's an ongoing process. Stay away from people who are not suitable for your health and fitness journey while constantly striving to maintain good thoughts, good words, and good deeds.

Chapter Two: Feed Your Mind, Body & Soul

More Than Just a Casual Knowledge of Food

Nutrition is an interesting subject. There are plenty of diets in the world, all claiming that their way is the best, but are they? People are very different. We all have a distinct genetic composition, cultural dietary variations, and individual body chemistry. People have different blood types, activity levels, circadian rhythms—the list goes on. What may be suitable for one person may be wrong for the next. For example, everybody acts and reacts differently to their surrounding environment, and we are each coded differently with a personal genetic makeup. Some of us may have grown up with strict dietary rules, including religious, moral, or specific food intolerances. For instance, many people cannot consume lactose, a sugar found in dairy. Lactose intolerance affects almost 65% of the world's population. [1]Other than food intolerances, food allergies and disease processes affect how and what you eat; something good for one person may not be ideal for someone else. It is necessary to choose what is chemically suitable for you; one size does not fit all.

How do you select a diet that will allow you to become fit and remain fit? Or a diet that is right for you and that you can adapt to your lifestyle? The first thing you need to ask yourself is what you like to eat, what you want to eat, and what you want to avoid. Let's break down the three classes of nutrients we need to ingest. No matter what dietary rules you wish to adopt, knowing what you are eating will help you make the right food choices.

Carbohydrates

Sugars are simple carbohydrates; various sugars make up complex carbohydrates. Both supply energy to your brain and other organs. Fruits and vegetables are filled with what is known as "good sugar." There are three types of sugars in fruit: fructose, glucose, and sucrose. Fructose and glucose are simple sugars, consisting of just one molecule called a

---

[1] Lukito W, Malik SG, Surono IS, Wahlqvist ML. From 'lactose intolerance' to 'lactose nutrition'. Asia Pac J Clin Nutr. 2015;24 Suppl 1:S1-8. doi: 10.6133/apjcn.2015.24.s1.01. PMID: 26715078.

monosaccharide, while sucrose is a disaccharide containing two molecules, which are the two simple sugars. Hence, sucrose comprises one glucose molecule and one fructose molecule.

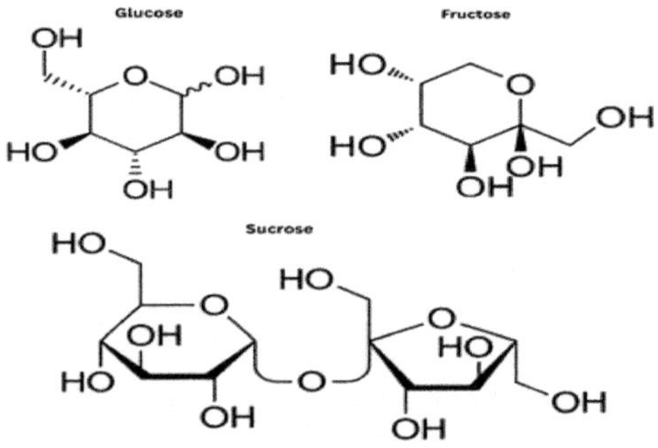

Eating fruits or vegetables supplies your body with good sugars while you ingest fiber and healthy vitamins and nutrients. Eating fruits and vegetables gives your body energy and can help you avoid chronic diseases like Type II diabetes. When you eat these natural carbohydrates, you are consuming healthy nutrition; the fruit or vegetable contains enough "filler," in the form of fiber, to prevent your body from overloading with sugar. This is not true when it comes to juicing your fruits.[2] While engaging in personal juicing, you are stripping away the fiber, which is important for

[2] Seino, Y., Iizuka, K., & Suzuki, A. (2021). Eating whole fruits, not drinking fruits juice, may reduce the risk of type 2 diabetes mellitus. *Journal of Diabetes Investigation.* https://doi.org/10.1111/jdi.13639

preventing Type II diabetes.[3] Natural, unprocessed foods have healthy safeguards built in, which come from years of evolution. Nature cannot be duplicated in the food lab. The natural protections found in foods are often removed as they are mass-produced.

The sugar in processed or junk food often contains sucrose, but it is refined in a laboratory and heavily packed into those treats. Another common processed sugar is high fructose corn syrup, a sweetener made from corn starch. These highly packed processed sugars overload your system. For example, an average-sized apple may contain 19 grams of sugar, whereas a glass of soda can contain anywhere from 35 to 39 grams of sugar. This is approximately double the amount of sugar typically found in nature, and this soda sugar most likely has been boiled and converted to supersaturated sucrose or high fructose corn syrup, the sugar that labs create and insert into these unhealthy snacks. With double the amount of sugar, it stands to reason that your pancreas, brain, and other organs are flooded with a spike in unhealthy energy levels. This puts an extra load on your system and makes it work twice as hard. Double the sugar,

---

[3] Weickert, M. O., & Pfeiffer, A. F. (2018). Impact of Dietary Fiber Consumption on Insulin Resistance and the Prevention of Type 2 Diabetes. *The Journal of Nutrition*, *148*(1), 7–12. https://doi.org/10.1093/jn/nxx008

without the fiber and nutrients, is a significant jolt to your body. This high energy demand, which overworks your essential organs, causes a sugar high followed by a sugar crash.

A little-known fact about eating junk food, especially candy and soft drinks, is that it can actually increase your low-density lipoproteins (LDL), also known as "bad cholesterol." All that sugar can raise your total cholesterol levels. Your liver produces more LDL from processed sugar, and that same sugar also lowers your high-density lipoproteins (HDL), or "good cholesterol," which helps absorb the LDL. The result? Higher LDL and a higher total cholesterol level. [4]Even though you may not be eating "bad fats" (discussed below), consuming "bad sugars" can dramatically affect your cholesterol levels.

Another common sugar is starch, which is found in foods such as pasta, corn, potatoes, and wheat. Starch is a polysaccharide molecule that contains multiple glucose units. The longer the carbohydrate molecule, the slower it digests, allowing the energy derived from starch to seep into

---

[4] DiNicolantonio, J. J., Lucan, S. C., & O'Keefe, J. H. (2016). The Evidence for Saturated Fat and for Sugar Related to Coronary Heart Disease. *Progress in Cardiovascular Diseases*, *58*(5), 464–472. https://doi.org/10.1016/j.pcad.2015.11.006

your system at a more gradual pace. A common practice is for marathon runners to eat a big pasta meal the night before a race. Starch, because of its slow digestive process, prevents sugar spikes.

Starch

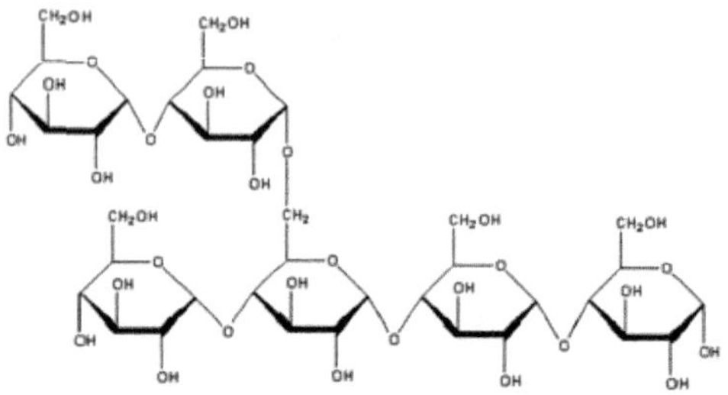

There are other types of carbohydrates, such as lactose found in milk products, stachyose found in beans, and galactose, which is structurally different from glucose by one chemical group, among many other sugars.

An important health and wellness rule is to consume natural sugars in their natural form. Processed sucrose, high-fructose corn syrup, and other lab-altered sugars are the ones you want to avoid. My intent in this discussion is not to inundate you with biochemistry; instead, I aim to provide a little knowledge about sugars and what to look for when choosing what to eat. Do not get caught up in the chemical structures; just focus on understanding the differences. It's important to always read food labels, which will offer a comparison between various products and provide the knowledge needed to make healthy choices.

Fats

Not all fat is bad for you; your body needs fats to survive and remain healthy. Fats are another source of energy and are essential for absorbing specific vitamins. Fats derived from fruits, vegetables, and nuts are considered "good fats," while fats originating from fast foods, lard, and anything made from trans fats are "bad fats." The critical question is: what type of fat will you eat?

Fat that remains solid at room temperature is saturated fat. The scientific nomenclature for saturated fats is "fully hydrogenated fatty acids." They are found in foods like butter, lard, coconut oil, dairy products, meats, and other sources. In the past, saturated fats have been implicated in raising cholesterol levels and increasing the risk of atherosclerosis, which has been linked to stroke and heart disease. However, the research world is now rethinking these past beliefs.[5],[6] They are examining the source of the saturated fat and what other ingredients may be included in the food product. Current recommendations state that you should limit saturated fat consumption to 8%–10% of your daily calorie intake.[7]

Saturated Fats

(No carbon double bonds)

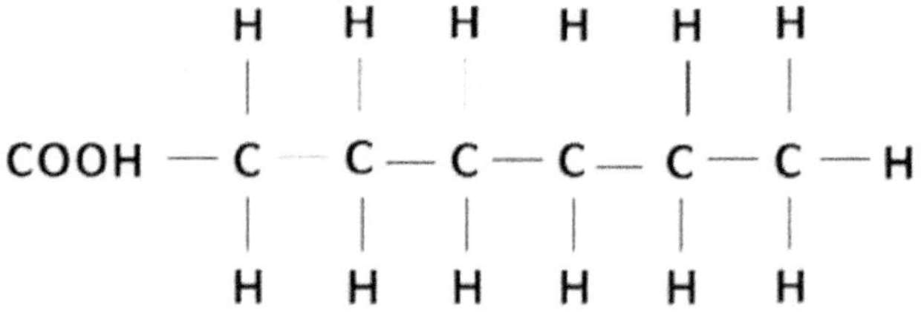

Monounsaturated fat is a molecule with one carbon double bond. This fat is commonly found in olive oil, canola

---

[5] Heileson JL. Dietary saturated fat and heart disease: a narrative review. Nutr Rev. 2020 Jun 1;78(6):474-485. doi: 10.1093/nutrit/nuz091. PMID: 31841151.

[6] Maki KC, Dicklin MR, Kirkpatrick CF. Saturated fats and cardiovascular health: Current evidence and controversies. J Clin Lipidol. 2021 Nov-Dec;15(6):765-772. doi: 10.1016/j.jacl.2021.09.049. Epub 2021 Oct 1. PMID: 34649831.

[7] Houston M. The relationship of saturated fats and coronary heart disease: fa(c)t or fiction? A commentary. Ther Adv Cardiovasc Dis. 2018 Feb;12(2):33-37. doi: 10.1177/1753944717742549. Epub 2017 Nov 19. PMID: 29153042; PMCID: PMC5933589.

oil, peanut oil, sesame oil, and safflower oil. It is also found in avocados, peanuts, and some nuts. Monounsaturated fats are considered the healthiest as they can help reduce cholesterol levels and provide nutrients to help nourish and develop your cells[8,9]. Oils rich in monounsaturated fats commonly contain vitamin E.

Monounsaturated fat is considered the healthiest oil to cook with and consume. It is a reasonably stable molecule that is excellent for heart health and does not cause free radicals to develop in your body. Free radicals are unstable atoms that can cause cell damage, leading to potential health issues such as DNA damage, aging, and even cancer. We'll discuss free radicals in further detail later in this book.

---

[8] Schwingshackl L, Hoffmann G. Monounsaturated fatty acids, olive oil and health status: a systematic review and meta-analysis of cohort studies. Lipids Health Dis. 2014 Oct 1;13:154. doi: 10.1186/1476-511X-13-154. PMID: 25274026; PMCID: PMC4198773.

[9] Gillingham LG, Harris-Janz S, Jones PJ. Dietary monounsaturated fatty acids are protective against metabolic syndrome and cardiovascular disease risk factors. Lipids. 2011 Mar;46(3):209-28. doi: 10.1007/s11745-010-3524-y. Epub 2011 Feb 10. PMID: 21308420.

Monounsaturated Fat

(1 carbon double bond)

Polyunsaturated fats are molecules that carry two or more carbon double bonds. They are found in foods such as canola oil, soybean oil, fatty fish, some nuts, and soybeans. Polyunsaturated fats, like monounsaturated fats, are regarded by researchers as fats that can help prevent heart disease by lowering total cholesterol[10].

Omega-3 fatty acids are a category of natural polyunsaturated fat that is beneficial for your health. There are three types of Omega-3 fatty acids: Alpha-linolenic acid, found in plant oils such as some nuts, canola oil, and flaxseed; and eicosapentaenoic acid and docosahexaenoic acid, both found in fish and seafood. Each of these Omega-3 fatty acids has shown evidence of reducing triglycerides, lowering blood pressure, and reducing blood clotting and inflammation throughout the body.

---

[10] Hooper L, Summerbell CD, Thompson R, Sills D, Roberts FG, Moore HJ, Davey Smith G. Reduced or modified dietary fat for preventing cardiovascular disease. Cochrane Database Syst Rev. 2012 May 16;2012(5):CD002137. doi: 10.1002/14651858.CD002137.pub3. PMID: 22592684; PMCID: PMC6486029.

Polyunsaturated Fat

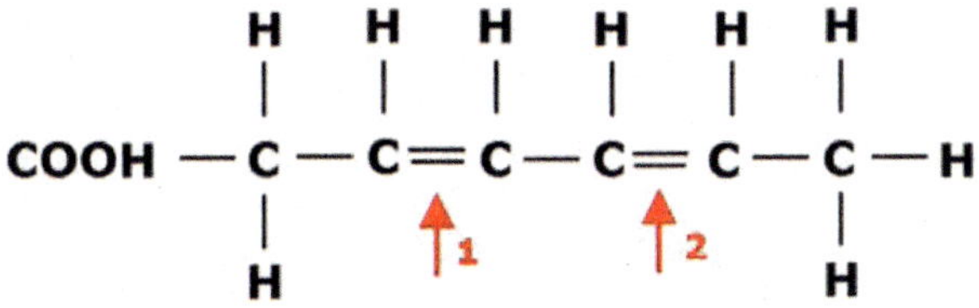

High polyunsaturated fat intake has been implicated in increasing susceptibility to some cancers[11, 12]. Polyunsaturated fats may cause a chain reaction in the body that produces free radicals, which, as discussed above, are unstable atoms that cause cell damage and lead to other potential health issues. Overuse of polyunsaturated fats has been linked to colon, breast, and some skin cancers.

There is controversy and competing opinions on which fat is healthiest to consume—polyunsaturated or saturated—and in what proportions. Depending on the scientist, some recommend cooking with polyunsaturated fats because they are healthier for the heart than saturated fats. Other scientists

---

[11] Roux-Levy C, Binquet C, Vaysse C, Scherrer ML, Ayav A, Ortega-Deballon P, Lakkis Z, Liu D, Deguelte S, Cottet V. Association between polyunsaturated fatty acids in adipose tissue and mortality of colorectal cancer patients. Nutrition. 2024 May;121:112358. doi: 10.1016/j.nut.2024.112358. Epub 2024 Jan 10. PMID: 38401197.

[12] Bartsch H, Nair J, Owen RW. Dietary polyunsaturated fatty acids and cancers of the breast and colorectum: emerging evidence for their role as risk modifiers. Carcinogenesis. 1999 Dec;20(12):2209-18. doi: 10.1093/carcin/20.12.2209. PMID: 10590211.

advocate limiting polyunsaturated fats because of the increased risk of free radicals, suggesting that saturated fats may be better as they can lower the risk of free radicals. Depending on the source, there is a degree of divergence of opinion and ongoing scientific debate. However, there is no argument that monounsaturated fats are the healthiest. Along with choosing nuts, avocados, and other natural sources of fats, always be sure of the quality and source of the fat you consume or cook with—read the labels.

Very Bad Fats

There is no controversy when it comes to trans fats; they are the worst type of fat you can consume. They are created in the lab when hydrogen is added to vegetable oil, allowing trans fats to exist in solid form at room temperature. The process is called hydrogenation and has been commonly used by the fast-food industry to produce cheaper cooking oil. It was also commonly found in baked goods, donuts, and other deep-fried foods. Trans fats increase your LDL (bad cholesterol) and lower your HDL (good cholesterol). As mentioned earlier, HDL absorbs LDL, so with lower levels of HDL, your LDL is not removed efficiently. Trans fats have also been found to promote tumor growth and limit your body's ability to fight cancer. This is a dietary source that all research shows is best to limit or avoid completely. New laws in the United States have been written to regulate trans fats.

In 2003, seventeen countries began banning or limiting the quantity of trans fats permitted in food preparation. Various countries have adopted a range of legal approaches, from restricting the amount of trans fats allowed in food products to creating a total trans fat ban. In 2003, the United States began requiring foods containing trans fats to be labeled. Over the next 16 years, trans fat laws progressed from mandatory labeling to strict limitations on their use. In 2019, the United States effectively banned trans fats in all food products.

Trans Fat

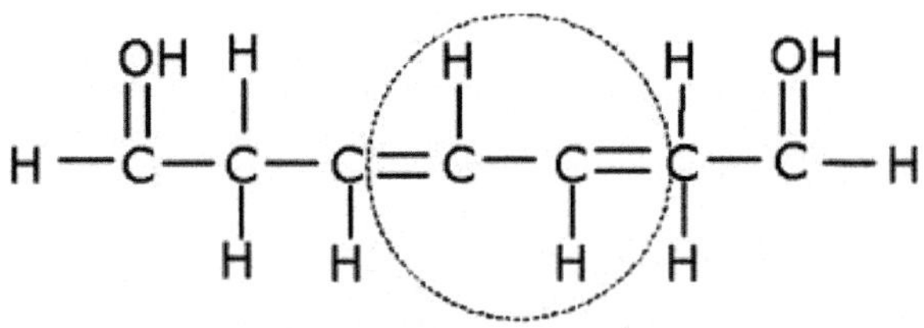

Because of the new anti-trans fat laws, another type of fat is making its way into the "cheap to produce yet bad for you" category: seed oil. In its most basic form, this type of fat is a polyunsaturated fat derived from vegetables and seeds. In the speedy yet cheap process of producing these oils, they are often made using chemical solvents instead of the healthier practice of crushing or squeezing the oil out of the seeds. During the refining process, these oils are stripped of their antioxidants, vitamins, and polyphenols, which are chemicals that help manage inflammation and protect you from oxidative stress. Seed oils are also bleached, refined, and chemically altered during preparation.

The eight seeds commonly used are corn oil, cottonseed, sunflower, safflower, peanut oil, rice bran, grapeseed oil, and rapeseed oil, known as the "Hateful Eight" in health guru circles. Seed oils are unhealthy because they are processed and used in pre-packaged and conventional foods. Many fast foods are prepared with seed oils, and unbeknownst to some health-conscious people, packaged health food snacks also contain seed oils.

Seed oil is also high in Omega-6 fatty acids, which are essential but should be consumed in lower amounts. Omega-6 increases inflammation and needs to be countered by Omega-3 fatty acids. The intake ratio of these two fatty acids can affect your health both positively and negatively. The dietary ratio of Omega-6 to Omega-3 is recommended to be 4:1 (four Omega-6 to one Omega-3) according to the Dietary Guidelines for Americans 2020–2025, issued by the United States Government. Some studies have shown that a ratio of

1:1 is healthier, as it decreases both atherosclerosis and chronic inflammation[13,14]. Seed oils in their purest form are not harmful to you; it is how they are processed, the foods they are found in, and their effect on your dietary fatty acid ratio that makes them unhealthy.

Protein

Protein is a large molecule that performs many important bodily functions. Thirty percent of your muscle tissue is protein. Protein is necessary for energy conversion, tissue repair, and nutrient absorption. Mammals, including humans, require 20 different amino acids to make up a protein molecule, and 9 of these 20 are characterized as "essential." Essential amino acids are not synthesized by the body, meaning they must be consumed through food, as we cannot produce these 9 amino acids ourselves. The essential amino acids are histidine, isoleucine, leucine, lysine, methionine, phenylalanine, threonine, tryptophan, and

---

[13] DiNicolantonio, J. J., & O'Keefe, J. H. (2018). Importance of maintaining a low omega–6/omega–3 ratio for reducing inflammation. *Open Heart*, *5*(2), e000946. https://doi.org/10.1136/openhrt-2018-000946

[14] Simopoulos, A. (2013). Dietary Omega-3 Fatty Acid Deficiency and High Fructose Intake in the Development of Metabolic Syndrome, Brain Metabolic Abnormalities, and Non-Alcoholic Fatty Liver Disease. *Nutrients*, *5*(8), 2901–2923. https://doi.org/10.3390/nu5082901

valine. Foods that contain all nine essential amino acids include beef, poultry, fish, eggs, dairy, soy, quinoa, and buckwheat. Other foods contain some essential amino acids, but not all. Vegans must follow a "whole-food vegan diet" to ensure they consume all nine essential amino acids. Unless vegans carefully select the right plants in a whole-food diet, they may miss out on critical amino acids.

The other 11 amino acids can be manufactured by your body and come from processes such as your internal recycling of dead cells. This recycling system is part of the body's normal and healthy life cycle.

The demand for protein varies depending on a person's body chemistry and physical activity. Exercise enthusiasts, athletes, and other highly active people have a greater demand for protein, as they metabolize and break down their tissue faster and more often, requiring protein for repair and replacement. As we build and maintain fitness, our demand for protein increases.

The average amount of protein required is 0.8 grams per kilogram of body weight per day. This varies depending on the individual's activity level. Someone who exercises regularly may require 1.2–1.7 grams of protein per kilogram of body weight.

Although meat is the easiest way to obtain protein, those on a primarily plant-based diet can still meet their protein needs. It takes a little more work and planning, but many nuts, plants, and legumes are rich in amino acids and proteins. Look at a cow or a horse as examples—neither of these muscular animals eats meat. Plant-based foods high in protein include beans, broccoli, peas, chickpeas, lentils, nuts, and seeds. If you choose to eat vegan, investigate the amount of protein in each plant you consume and ensure it matches your desired and needed protein intake. The practice of what is called "protein complementation" is important for vegans. It means combining different plant-based foods in your diet, including nuts, grains, legumes, vegetables, and fruits, to ensure you receive all nine essential amino acids.

Knowing what you eat is essential to being fit and healthy. Regardless of the type of diet or eating habits you choose, it is critical to understand the importance of carbohydrates, fats, and proteins. These macronutrients are the cornerstone of every diet. It is important to read labels and question what is in your food. Healthy decisions can be made when you know exactly what you are consuming and its effects on your body. You cannot exercise your way out of a bad diet; you need to eat healthily and consciously, with more than just a casual knowledge of food.

Chapter Three: Diets and Food Options

There are plenty of diets, styles, and ways you are told that you "should be eating." The marketplace offers many options, each claiming that their way is the best. If that were true, why are over 70% of Americans considered overweight or obese? National Institutes of Health surveys have found that population obesity rates have tripled in the last 60 years. The Wall Street Journal has reported that the diet industry collects 76 billion dollars annually. This makes us wonder if fitness is really their goal or if they wish to keep the public confused and dependent, allowing the diet industry to reap the resulting financial windfall.

Most people do not know how to lose weight in the long term or how to keep the weight off. Many fad diets are often sold as short-term ways to "lose weight quickly." Our mission is to become and stay fit, which is about playing the long game—whether you are considered obese, have "love handles," or are looking to gain weight. Diet schemes set you up for long-term failure; they create rebound, depression, and exhaustion. They are not suitable for your system or your mental wellness. The plan is to think long-term and develop strategies to become and stay fit. What you eat is a big part of your fitness, and various diets are discussed in this chapter.

Below is a simplistic breakdown of some of the more common diets and eating approaches. Other diets on the market may or may not work, but the goal should be long-term success, not a quick fix. We are looking for a new way of life that will offer you a lifetime of fitness. A complete plan is needed so that when you celebrate a holiday and go off your "new regular way of eating," you do not get down on yourself; you pick right back up and move on. That is why the first topic will include some background on fasting.

The Benefits of Fasting

Fasting is not starving; instead, it is avoiding food for a certain period to take advantage of potential health benefits. Some people can and do fast for days, while others participate in intermittent fasting, which consists of fasting for a specific number of hours and then repeating the process a few days later.

Fasting promotes glucose control by reducing insulin resistance. Multiple studies confirm the positive benefits of fasting for both glucose and insulin.[1,2] When fasting, your body decreases insulin resistance, increasing your body's sensitivity to insulin. This allows glucose to be transported from the bloodstream to cells more efficiently.

Fasting also reduces inflammation, which in turn helps prevent chronic diseases. Many disease processes stem from chronic inflammation. A study published in the journal Nutrition[3] explained how intermittent fasting can reduce the prevalence of an inflammatory marker in your body called C-reactive protein. C-reactive protein is produced by the liver in response to inflammation and is an important blood test marker used to identify acute inflammation.

Alternate-day fasting (ADF) may enhance your heart health by lowering blood pressure, triglycerides, and cholesterol levels. A 2020 study found that ADF is related to

---

[1] Teong, X.T., Liu, K., Vincent, A.D. et al. Intermittent fasting plus early time-restricted eating versus calorie restriction and standard care in adults at risk of type 2 diabetes: a randomized controlled trial. Nat Med 29, 963–972 (2023).

[2] Vasim I, Majeed CN, DeBoer MD. Intermittent Fasting and Metabolic Health. Nutrients. 2022 Jan 31;14(3):631. doi: 10.3390/nu14030631. PMID: 35276989; PMCID: PMC8839325.

[3] Wang X, Yang Q, Liao Q, Li M, Zhang P, Santos HO, Kord-Varkaneh H, Abshirini M. Effects of intermittent fasting diets on plasma concentrations of inflammatory biomarkers: A systematic review and meta-analysis of randomized controlled trials. Nutrition. 2020 Nov-Dec;79-80:110974. doi: 10.1016/j.nut.2020.110974. Epub 2020 Aug 12. PMID: 32947129

weight reduction, lowered risks of weight regain, and relative lean body mass preservation compared to continuous energy restriction.[4] Other scientific papers explain how weight loss and weight control can benefit from fasting.[5] Fasting can also support a decrease in insulin levels and an increase in Human Growth Hormone release,[6] improve brain function,[7] and aid cancer prevention[8] while enhancing the benefits of chemotherapy.[9] While fasting offers many benefits, it is important to know what you are

---

[4] Park J, Seo YG, Paek YJ, Song HJ, Park KH, Noh HM. Effect of alternate-day fasting on obesity and cardiometabolic risk: A systematic review and meta-analysis. Metabolism. 2020 Oct;111:154336. doi: 10.1016/j.metabol.2020.154336. Epub 2020 Aug 7. PMID: 32777443.

[5] Zhang Q, Zhang C, Wang H, Ma Z, Liu D, Guan X, Liu Y, Fu Y, Cui M, Dong J. Intermittent Fasting versus Continuous Calorie Restriction: Which Is Better for Weight Loss? Nutrients. 2022 Apr 24;14(9):1781. doi: 10.3390/nu14091781. PMID: 35565749; PMCID: PMC9099935.

[6] Brocchi A, Rebelos E, Dardano A, Mantuano M, Daniele G. Effects of Intermittent Fasting on Brain Metabolism. Nutrients. 2022 Mar 17;14(6):1275. doi: 10.3390/nu14061275. PMID: 35334932; PMCID: PMC8954770.

[7] Elesawy BH, Raafat BM, Muqbali AA, Abbas AM, Sakr HF. The Impact of Intermittent Fasting on Brain-Derived Neurotrophic Factor, Neurotrophin 3, and Rat Behavior in a Rat Model of Type 2 Diabetes Mellitus. Brain Sci. 2021 Feb 15;11(2):242. doi: 10.3390/brainsci11020242. PMID: 33671898; PMCID: PMC7918995.

[8] Katherine K Clifton MD, Cynthia X. Ma MD, PhD, Luigi Fontana MD, PhD, FRACP, Lindsay L. Peterson MD, MSC. Intermittent fasting in the prevention and treatment of cancer. CA A Cancer Journal for Clinicians, August 12, 2021

[9] Sadeghian M, Rahmani S, Khalesi S, Hejazi E. A review of fasting effects on the response of cancer to chemotherapy. Clin Nutr. 2021 Apr;40(4):1669-1681. doi: 10.1016/j.clnu.2020.10.037. Epub 2020 Oct 23. PMID: 33153820.

doing and how to fast safely. If you are under the care of a physician for an illness, be sure to include your doctor in the decision-making process.

When incorporating fasting into your lifestyle, it is always best to start slow. This means starting with an introductory 12-hour fast. It is not much of a fast, but it will allow you to experience what may be in store when attempting longer fasts. While fasting, you should only consume water. If you fast for days, you can consume other zero-calorie beverages, but water should be your primary intake. The easiest way to begin a fast is not to eat anything after your last meal and wait until lunch the next day to eat again. For example, when you are ready to try a 16-hour fast, you can finish your dinner at 8:00 pm and then not eat again until noon the following day. This will give you a 16-hour fast, with most of the time spent sleeping and only a few hours to manage the following day.

Many have found that the "5:2 Method" is a healthy intermittent fasting pattern. This entails eating regularly for five days and fasting twice weekly. Be sure to spread the two days out during the week to create a balanced seven days of eating and fasting. For example, fast on Monday and Thursday or Tuesday and Friday, so you do not fast two days in a row. A 16-hour fast is sufficient time to allow your body chemistry to reset and heal. Some people may attempt longer fasts lasting multiple days. These longer fasts facilitate anti-aging and improved immune response. I recommend starting with intermittent fasting before attempting any long-term fast. Overall, intermittent fasting twice a week for 16 hours offers dramatic health benefits. Again, if you are on any medication, it is always best to consult your physician before attempting a fast.

Intermittent fasting is also a great way to recover from a night of partying, a holiday celebration, or any time you fall off your healthy eating pattern. I want to be realistic in this book, and slip-ups will, of course, occur. It's essential to get back on your fitness plan, and starting with a fast is an easy way to reset and clean up your system.

Various Diets

The following provides a simple analysis of some of the more popular diets. I am only introducing each diet and providing documentation on the claims they support. If you choose to follow any of these diets, it is highly recommended that you investigate further and delve deeper into each one. We will only touch on each of them here. Remember, to stay fit over 50, it is important to watch everything you eat and be mindful of consuming enough carbohydrates, fats, and proteins, especially the essential amino acids, as outlined in the previous chapter.

Vegan Diet

A vegan diet is always an excellent choice for health or social reasons. There are variations that a vegan purist might not agree with. Examples include pescatarians, individuals who eat a vegetarian diet and fish; lacto-ovo vegetarians, who allow eggs and milk; and flexitarians, whose diet is primarily vegetarian but includes some animal products. The most extreme is a raw vegetarian, where all foods are eaten raw, not cooked or steamed. I am offering no social judgment on eating animals; that is up to you to decide. Instead, I am discussing some essential practices that anyone following a vegetarian diet should include.

As discussed previously, proteins include nine essential amino acids necessary for humans to consume. Contrary to conventional thinking, protein can be obtained through the strict consumption of plants. Some muscular bodybuilders compete while following a pure vegan diet. Weightlifters have a high metabolic demand for protein, which helps them repair and recover from their workouts. However, vegan bodybuilders do not eat meat, providing evidence that sufficient protein levels can be obtained from plants, regardless of your activity level.

Anyone eating a vegan diet must be aware of what they are eating and ensure they are getting all the necessary vitamins, minerals, and amino acids. You cannot just eat plants and assume you have a healthy diet; rather, you need to follow a "whole-food plant-based diet." This form of vegan eating ensures you are getting all your protein, fats, and carbohydrates. It requires you to plan, select, and analyze everything. These meals are usually rich with many different types of consumable plants. Once you learn this process, it can become easy to choose foods you enjoy that also provide complete nutrition. It is vital to invest some time in researching and understanding the foods you need to consume.

As with any diet, stay away from overly processed foods and focus on the quality of what you are eating. Believe it or not, there are boxed, over-processed "dessert foods" that are vegan. Avoid eating excess highly marketed soy products, which are common in "replacement meat" foods. These products often contain unhealthy fillers such as corn, gluten, and highly processed legumes. Soy products were once believed to lower testosterone levels and increase estrogen levels, but these myths have been debunked. However, there are still questions about the relationship between soy and thyroid issues,[10] although more studies are necessary.

A vegan diet is extremely healthy, but you must ensure you get all nine amino acids. Follow a whole-food vegan diet to guarantee you are getting all the necessary nutrients.

---

[10] D'Adamo CR, Sahin A. Soy foods and supplementation: a review of commonly perceived health benefits and risks. Altern Ther Health Med. 2014 Winter;20 Suppl 1:39-51. PMID: 24473985.

Keto Diet

The keto diet, more correctly called the ketogenic diet, is where low amounts of sugar are consumed, and fat becomes the body's primary energy source. With the decrease in carbohydrate intake, the body enters a constant state of ketosis. This occurs when your liver processes fats into ketones, which then become the body's source of energy.

As the body remains in ketosis, blood sugar and insulin levels are reduced. To remain in ketosis, sugar intake needs to be reduced to 20-50 grams per day. It is also important not to overindulge in protein, as excess protein can be converted to sugar. If carbohydrate consumption increases while on a keto diet, the body will leave ketosis, and all the benefits of this eating style will be lost. It will then be nothing more than a high-fat diet.

One key benefit of the keto diet is reducing heart disease risk.[11] This occurs as the keto diet can reduce excess body weight, increase HDL cholesterol, and reduce blood

---

[11] Cicero AF, Benelli M, Brancaleoni M, Dainelli G, Merlini D, Negri R. Middle and Long-Term Impact of a Very Low-Carbohydrate Ketogenic Diet on Cardiometabolic Factors: A Multi-Center, Cross-Sectional, Clinical Study. High Blood Press Cardiovasc Prev. 2015 Dec;22(4):389-94. doi: 10.1007/s40292-015-0096-1. Epub 2015 May 19. PMID: 25986079; PMCID: PMC4666896.

pressure. As discussed earlier, higher HDL levels will absorb LDLs and ultimately lower your total cholesterol.

Reducing blood sugar levels will also reduce insulin levels, a significant benefit for preventing Type II diabetes.[12] The pancreas will be well-rested because it is not inundated with carbohydrates, and not overtaxing this organ will reduce the risk of developing pancreatic diseases.

Other benefits of the keto diet may include improved cancer prevention,[13] as the diet may slow the growth of tumors, reduce seizure activity, help with Parkinson's symptoms,[14] and slow the progression of Alzheimer's disease.[15] Healthy fats are good for the body, and their benefits are recognized scientifically.

---

[12] Boden G, Sargrad K, Homko C, Mozzoli M, Stein TP. Effect of a low-carbohydrate diet on appetite, blood glucose levels, and insulin resistance in obese patients with type 2 diabetes. Ann Intern Med. 2005 Mar 15;142(6):403-11. doi: 10.7326/0003-4819-142-6-200503150-00006. PMID: 15767618.

[13] Kosinski C, Jornayvaz FR. Effects of Ketogenic Diets on Cardiovascular Risk Factors: Evidence from Animal and Human Studies. Nutrients. 2017 May 19;9(5):517. doi: 10.3390/nu9050517. PMID: 28534852; PMCID: PMC5452247.

[14] Phillips MCL, Murtagh DKJ, Gilbertson LJ, Asztely FJS, Lynch CDP. Low-fat versus ketogenic diet in Parkinson's disease: A pilot randomized controlled trial. Mov Disord. 2018 Aug;33(8):1306-1314. doi: 10.1002/mds.27390. Epub 2018 Aug 11. Erratum in: Mov Disord. 2019 Jan;34(1):157. PMID: 30098269; PMCID: PMC6175383.

[15] Włodarek D. Role of Ketogenic Diets in Neurodegenerative Diseases (Alzheimer's Disease and Parkinson's Disease). Nutrients.

Some downsides to the keto diet, especially if not followed properly, include decreased mental acuity, reduced exercise performance, and irritability in the early days of starting this diet. The process of beginning a keto diet is labeled the "transitory period," as your system acclimates to reduced sugar levels. Participants in the keto diet also need to be wary of overconsuming deli or cold-cut meats, as these foods are high in nitrates, sodium, and other preservatives. I always recommend paying attention to the source of your food and being cautious with processed meals—"always read the labels" is a piece of advice that bears repeating.

If you wish to try the keto diet, further research into this eating style is necessary. You must consume healthy fats such as high-quality meats, fish, nuts, eggs, and oils. You can even follow a keto diet while being vegan.[16] This is a complex way of eating, but it can be accomplished without animal products. Do your research, know what you are doing, and speak with someone who is knowledgeable about how to eat keto while remaining vegan.

2019 Jan 15;11(1):169. doi: 10.3390/nu11010169. PMID: 30650523; PMCID: PMC6356942.

[16] Michael Guadagnino, BS, DC. Yes! You can eat a Vegan Keto Diet.www.DrGuadBlog.com March 14, 2023

If you enjoy a drink from time to time and follow the keto diet, be sure to read the labels. Most alcohol is high in sugar, but some spirits fit within the keto diet. You can drink, but it's important to know which beverages are keto-friendly—they do exist.

While following the keto diet, it's also a good idea to regularly monitor yourself with an over-the-counter self-check ketosis kit. This is the only way to ensure you are in a state of ketosis. You can test your blood, breath, or urine. With the amount of research and anecdotal evidence supporting the keto diet, it has kept countless people healthy and fit. It may seem odd to someone initially introduced to a high-fat, low-carb diet that it is healthy. That's because it breaks the social norms that most of us have lived by. However, it makes physiological sense when the diet is broken down and explained.

Mediterranean Diet

As the name implies, this diet is inspired by the foods and choices familiar to those living in Mediterranean areas: Spain, southern Italy, Crete, and Greece. It is no coincidence that these populations are considered olive-growing cultures, as the primary source of fat in a Mediterranean diet is monounsaturated olive oil. As discussed earlier, olive oil is the healthiest choice for cooking.

The Mediterranean diet focuses on plant-based meals, including fruits, vegetables, nuts, legumes, grains, and seeds. It allows for moderate consumption of animal products, including eggs, fish, and meats. Red meat is restricted, with fish and poultry being the preferred choices. Some dairy products are included, but generally in the form of cheeses. Wine may be consumed with meals, and fruit is a typical dessert.

Like most other high-quality diets, the Mediterranean diet recommends avoiding processed foods, high sodium, refined sugars, fatty foods, and saturated fats. Instead, it focuses on natural, plant-based foods with a moderate amount of healthy animal products.

There have been quantifiable benefits associated with the Mediterranean diet, as it has been ranked a top diet by U.S. News & World Report six times. Studies have shown that people experience better sleep[17] with this diet, and improved sleep is one of the critical factors in health and

---

[17] Scoditti E, Tumolo MR, Garbarino S. Mediterranean Diet on Sleep: A Health Alliance. Nutrients. 2022 Jul 21;14(14):2998. doi: 10.3390/nu14142998. PMID: 35889954; PMCID: PMC9318336.

tissue repair. People also experience less inflammation,[18] and there is a lower risk of heart disease and overall cardiovascular disease in females.[19] A key factor is that the Mediterranean diet lowers LDLs. A large study reported in 2023, involving 60,000 participants, showed a decreased risk of dementia,[20] and a smaller study demonstrated that it may boost mental health.[21] A 2023 paper also suggested that the Mediterranean diet may increase overall life expectancy.[22]

There are many benefits to the Mediterranean diet. It's not as restrictive as some other diets and uses a lot of common sense, focusing on consuming more plants and

---

[18] Itsiopoulos C, Mayr HL, Thomas CJ. The anti-inflammatory effects of a Mediterranean diet: a review. Curr Opin Clin Nutr Metab Care. 2022 Nov 1;25(6):415-422. doi: 10.1097/MCO.0000000000000872. Epub 2022 Aug 30. PMID: 36039924.

[19] Pant A, Gribbin S, McIntyre D, et al. Primary prevention of cardiovascular disease in women with a Mediterranean diet: systematic review and meta-analysis. Heart 2023;109:1208-1215.

[20] Shannon, O.M., Ranson, J.M., Gregory, S. et al. Mediterranean diet adherence is associated with lower dementia risk, independent of genetic predisposition: findings from the UK Biobank prospective cohort study. BMC Med 21, 81 (2023).

[21] Jessica Raves, Janet Schloss, David Sibbritt. The effects of Mediterranean diet on the symptoms of depressed young males. The American Journal of Clinical Nutrition. Volume 116, Issue 2, P572-580 August 2022

[22] Shan Z, Wang F, Li Y, et al. Healthy Eating Patterns and Risk of Total and Cause-Specific Mortality. JAMA Intern Med. 2023;183(2):142–153. doi:10.1001/jamainternmed.2022.6117

avoiding processed foods. Many people worldwide are unfamiliar with the Mediterranean way of eating, but those originating from Mediterranean populations may already be eating something close to this type of diet. A few tweaks to their eating habits could easily align them with the Mediterranean diet.

The Paleo Diet

The Paleo diet is centered around what humans may have eaten during the Paleolithic Era. It emphasizes fruits, vegetables, fish, nuts, eggs, seeds, and lean meats. This diet is based on the belief that early humans consumed foods they hunted or foraged. The diet avoids foods that became popular after the development of farming around 10,000 years ago, including legumes, grains, and dairy.

Supporters of the Paleo diet claim that it can reduce inflammation, increase energy, improve weight loss, and stabilize blood sugar. They also claim it can reduce the risk of chronic diseases.

A 2015 study[23] illustrated that a Paleo diet may provide short-term benefits with weight loss, blood pressure

---

[23] Manheimer EW, van Zuuren EJ, Fedorowicz Z, Pijl H. Paleolithic nutrition for metabolic syndrome: systematic review and meta-analysis. Am J Clin Nutr. 2015 Oct;102(4):922-32. doi:

stabilization, improved HDL levels, and stabilized glucose levels. Another smaller study[24] showed that the Paleo diet may help reduce the risk of chronic diseases.

Since the Paleo diet is somewhat restrictive, it is important to ensure you consume all the necessary vitamins, amino acids, and fats. Some claims suggest that due to its restrictive nature, the diet may result in vitamin D and calcium deficiencies. Additionally, a study tied the Paleo diet to altered levels of gut microbiota and higher levels of trimethylamine N-oxide (TMAO),[25] which is associated with cardiovascular disease. Don't jump into any eating style just because it is trendy. Research it, understand it, and follow good guidelines.

Good Ol' Portion Control Diet

"Portion control diet" is a catch-all phrase but one that has made many companies wealthy, either by selling pre-packaged foods or branded calorie-counting diets. Some of

---

10.3945/ajcn.115.113613. Epub 2015 Aug 12. PMID: 26269362; PMCID: PMC4588744.

[24] de Menezes, E.V.A., Sampaio, H.A.d.C., Carioca, A.A.F. et al. Influence of Paleolithic diet on anthropometric markers in chronic diseases: systematic review and meta-analysis. Nutr J 18, 41 (2019)

[25] Genoni, A., Christophersen, C.T., Lo, J. et al. Long-term Paleolithic diet is associated with lower resistant starch intake, different gut microbiota composition and increased serum TMAO concentrations. Eur J Nutr 59, 1845–1858 (2020).

the more popular "diets" are simply forms of forced portion control. These diets ensure you don't overindulge in sugars or fats. Losing weight requires living on a calorie deficit. Simply put, you have to consume fewer calories than you expend each day. In Chapter 9: Incidentals, I discuss how your body burns calories daily and how being in a calorie deficit leads to weight loss. Exercise, walking to work, and doing daily chores all expend a certain number of calories. Eating fewer calories helps you lose weight.

If you don't want to lose weight but want to gain muscle or stay lean, portion control can help you reach your goals by balancing your protein, carbohydrate, and fat intake. Unlike the other diets discussed in this chapter, portion control offers a diverse range of food options. As I've said many times, read labels—this is the only way to know exactly what you are consuming.

A standard method used by many dieticians and food publications for portion control is as follows:

Fill half your plate with vegetables, a quarter with lean protein, and the last quarter with carbohydrates. The critical point is to ensure you don't have an enormous plate or a pile of food on your plate. This would negate portion control. It goes back to the first part, good ol' common sense.

As has been stressed many times, when choosing a specific diet, know what you are doing or ask someone who knows. There are plenty of books, nutrition articles, and videos to consult. If you speak with someone, it is important that they have some level of authority on nutrition.

Knowing fats, proteins, and carbohydrates helps you to make good choices. Staying away from over-processed or highly preserved food is extremely important to being and staying fit. Regardless of how you eat, you need to consider these lessons and be sure you are getting the right amount and type of macro and micronutrients into your diet. Your goals could be weight loss, more strength, or overall health as you drive yourself to be fit over 50. Whichever way you choose to eat, make sure you eat in a way that offers you the best diet and food options.

Chapter Four:

Supplements?

How About a Real-World Encyclopedia of Supplements

The level of nourishment in today's food supply has been considerably stripped away compared to years past. Our agricultural processes, which produce vast amounts of food, tend to disrupt the soil's health. Modern irrigation, fertilization, and harvesting disturb microbial activity in the soil and reduce the absorption of nutrients into plants, including those consumed by livestock. If you strive to be fit, you will want to eat a clean diet, which includes meals that are less processed and comprise large quantities of fresh fruits and vegetables. The nutritional value of today's food may not be exactly what is perceived.

Organic farming has demonstrated higher levels of nutrients in foods than non-organic farming. However, organic farming still lacks the nutritional value found in organic farming years ago. High demand, speed, and the need for profits have affected soil nutrients in both organic and non-organic farming. It is true that organic food has lower levels of pesticides, lower levels of toxic metals such as cadmium, and higher levels of antioxidants than non-organic food. Animals raised for meat and fed on organic farming products will also have higher nutritional value because they consume better-quality food. Organic farming of animals generally includes vaccinating them against disease; however, there is no present scientific evidence suggesting that human consumption of vaccinated animals is harmful.

One way to combat the issue of nutrient-depleted food is to use supplements. It was discovered during the recent COVID-19 pandemic that many people suffer from a vitamin D deficiency.[1] [2] If Americans live in a society where dairy and other sources of vitamin D are so readily consumed, why do we have such a deficiency in this vitamin? Another question to ask is, what other vitamins and nutrients are we unknowingly deficient in? Studies

---

[1] Amiel A. Dror, Nicole Morozov, Amani Daoud, Yoav Namir, Orly Yakir, Yair Shachar, Mark Lifshitz, Ella Segal, Lior Fisher, Matti Mizrachi, Netanel Eisenbach, Doaa Rayan, Maayan Gruber. Pre-infection 25-hydroxyvitamin D3 levels and association with severity of COVID-19 illness. PLOS One. February 3, 2022

[2] Sartini M, Del Puente F, Oliva M, Carbone A, Bobbio N, Schinca E, Giribone L, Cristina ML. Preventive Vitamin D Supplementation and Risk for COVID-19 Infection: A Systematic Review and Meta-Analysis. Nutrients. 2024 Feb 28;16(5):679. doi: 10.3390/nu16050679. PMID: 38474807; PMCID: PMC10935157.

conducted during the pandemic revealed that our food is not as nutrient-rich as we once thought. Deductive reasoning would suggest that we are eating nutrient-stripped food and not getting our recommended daily allowance (RDA) of vitamins, minerals, or antioxidants. Taking supplements is a more reliable way to know what nutrients you are consuming and at what levels.

Knowing how to take supplements is as important as using them. It is paramount that supplements are absorbed into your body and do not end up in your toilet. You must consciously take advantage of your body's digestive chemistry to absorb these supplements rather than have them pass through your kidneys or colon without entering your body's cells.

A good practice is to ingest fat-soluble supplements with a meal containing fats and take water-soluble supplements with a meal low in fat. A meal with fats can include olive oil, avocado, eggs, meats, and similar foods. Non-fat meals can include pasta, rice, vegetables, and other carbohydrates, including cereals. As you eat a meal, your digestive system absorbs the select macronutrients. The key is to ingest a similar supplement with or after such a meal to allow for complete and prompt digestion; otherwise, the supplement may pass through without becoming part of your metabolic process.

Fat-soluble vitamins include A, D, E, and K, while water-soluble vitamins are Bs and C. Other important supplements, including CoQ10, Curcumin, Resveratrol, and Omega-3 fatty acids, also fall under the fat-soluble classification.

Water-soluble minerals are best consumed in their natural organic state. For example, a mineral such as calcium should be consumed in an organic form. Attempting to obtain calcium from inorganic sources such as antacids will not achieve that goal. Calcium needs to be digested in an acidic environment. The primary action of antacids is to neutralize an acidic stomach so the user does not suffer from heartburn. If you are taking an antacid as a source of calcium, realize that this calcium will now be in a non-acidic (neutral to basic) environment and not absorbed into your cells. We'll discuss calcium supplementation later in this chapter, under the section on minerals, including better forms of consumption such as calcium citrate and the importance of ingesting vitamin D along with calcium.

I do not support taking multivitamins, as they contain a mixture of fat-soluble and water-soluble vitamins in one solution. Mixing the two types of vitamins impedes the absorption of any of them. It is best to take a fat-soluble vitamin with a meal containing eggs, olive oil, or avocado and a water-soluble vitamin with fruit juice, pasta, or rice. Multivitamins mix the two soluble vitamin forms together, which is not optimal for absorption.

Skeptics who do not support taking vitamins often make baseless claims. These individuals may or may not be in the healthcare field, and their opinions are often based on limited information. Their biggest gripe usually centers around the body's ability to digest supplements. While they are partially correct, their arguments cease to hold water in cases where you consume a "like vitamin with a like meal." Their second concern, which is also partially valid, questions the quality of supplements you may be ingesting. Supplements formulated with many fillers are a poor choice and ineffective because their absorption and chemical makeup are greatly lacking.

Skeptics also scrutinize a practice known as "megadosing." Megadosing is something recommended in a more clinical setting, not for general health and fitness. Skeptics claim that most of the "megadose" is passed through the body without absorption, and they may be right. Megadosing is not the focus of being fit over 50, and I would not recommend megadosing vitamins unless prescribed by your physician. Often, it is used to treat a specific disease or disorder. It is always recommended to use high-quality supplements, take them with the right foods, and stay within safe consumption parameters, which negates the skeptics' arguments. It is important to remember that supplementation is not to be used in place of a nourishing diet. The key word is "supplement," as these are used to supplement or enhance your overall nutrition.

Supplements can also strengthen your immune system; do not confuse this with meaning you will not get sick. People become run down, are exposed to certain elements, and have other reasons for illness. The correct amount of vitamins, minerals, or other supplements allows your immune, nervous, and other bodily systems to work at a higher level. Exposure to a cold virus while taking zinc and vitamin C may not prevent the cold, but it will allow your immune system to function at its highest level, helping to relieve symptoms and enabling your body to rid itself of these infectious diseases.

There are other important supplements, such as CoQ10, which is an antioxidant that your body produces naturally. However, in the case of those who are physically compromised and as people age, the body has difficulty manufacturing it. A 2020 study stated that CoQ10 may help those suffering from heart failure[3] and possibly high blood pressure.[4] This supplement, like others, does not cure a problem but enhances the body's ability to respond, adapt, and become healthier.

The following is a breakdown of individual vitamins, minerals, and certain antioxidants. The body needs to be in a state of homeostatic balance, which includes the regulation of important vitamins and minerals. Homeostatic balance is achieved by the synergistic operation of all of the body's systems: cardiovascular, lymphatic, nervous, respiratory, integumentary, endocrine, urinary, musculoskeletal, immune, reproductive, and gastrointestinal.

The following is a general, real-life explanation of each type of supplement with an easy-access chart below each

---

[3] Di Lorenzo A, Iannuzzo G, Parlato A, Cuomo G, Testa C, Coppola M, D'Ambrosio G, Oliviero DA, Sarullo S, Vitale G, Nugara C, Sarullo FM, Giallauria F. Clinical Evidence for Q10 Coenzyme Supplementation in Heart Failure: From Energetics to Functional Improvement. J Clin Med. 2020 Apr 27;9(5):1266. doi: 10.3390/jcm9051266. PMID: 32349341; PMCID: PMC7287951.

[4] Tabrizi R, Akbari M, Sharifi N, Lankarani KB, Moosazadeh M, Kolahdooz F, Taghizadeh M, Asemi Z. The Effects of Coenzyme Q10 Supplementation on Blood Pressures Among Patients with Metabolic Diseases: A Systematic Review and Meta-analysis of Randomized Controlled Trials. High Blood Press Cardiovasc Prev. 2018 Mar;25(1):41-50. doi: 10.1007/s40292-018-0247-2. Epub 2018 Jan 12. PMID: 29330704.

section. There are entire books written about each vitamin; here, you will receive general yet important information. Possessing knowledge about supplements will give you a basic understanding of these adjuncts, which can be vitally important to include with meals. I cannot stress this enough: if you are taking any medication, you should consult with your prescribing physician before taking any supplements, nor am I suggesting that you self-treat any condition with supplements.

The Fat-Soluble Vitamins

Vitamin A is essential for vision, growth, cell division, immunity, and reproduction. It also has important antioxidant properties. In foods, vitamin A is found in spinach, dairy, and liver. Foods high in beta-carotene, such as carrots, cantaloupe, and green leafy vegetables, allow your body to metabolize the beta-carotene and convert it to vitamin A. The RDA is 900 mcg for adult men and 700 mcg for adult women. Megadosing on vitamin A can have adverse health effects.

Vitamin D is essential for building and maintaining bone health by playing a role as a catalyst for calcium absorption. Vitamin D also acts as an anti-inflammatory antioxidant, supports your immune system, and improves brain cell activity and muscle function. Vitamin D can be taken in two forms: D2 or D3. D2 is a non-animal product, while D3 is derived from animal products and is more effective for absorption. Foods high in vitamin D include liver, fatty fish, egg yolk, fish oils, mushrooms, tofu, and spinach. The RDA for Vitamin D is 400 IU for infants, 600 IU for ages 1–70, and 800 IU for those over 70. Sunlight is also an excellent source of vitamin D, as light converts cholesterol to vitamin D.

Vitamin E is necessary for vision, reproduction, and blood, brain, and skin health. It also acts as an antioxidant. Vitamin E can be found in meat, dairy, olive oil, and leafy green vegetables. The RDA for Vitamin E is 15 mg per day.

Fat Soluble Vitamins		
Vitamin	**Necessity**	**RDA**
A	vision, growth cell division, immunity reproduction	900 mcg adult men 700 mcg adult women
D	building & maintaining bone health anti-inflammatory antioxidant aiding calcium absorption immune support improves brain and muscle function	600 IU ages 1 -70 800 Iu over 70 D3 better source than D2
E	vision, reproduction blood, brain & skin health antioxidant	15 mg
K	Blood clotting, bone health	30ug - 90ug

Vitamin K is a crucial nutrient for building healthy bones and is essential for blood clotting. Vitamin K comes from two sources: K1 and K2. Vitamin K1 is commonly found in plants such as green leafy vegetables, whereas K2 is less common and found in fermented products and some animal foods. The bacteria in your gut also produce K2. There is no RDA for Vitamin K, and the recommended "adequate amounts" range from 30 mcg to 90 mcg, depending on age. Unless you have a genetic disorder or a condition that alters your gut bacteria, this is one vitamin you generally do not need to worry about supplementing as long as you eat a healthy diet.

The Water-Soluble Vitamins

Vitamin C is an important nutrient for forming blood vessels, cartilage, muscles, and collagen, and it is necessary for your body's healing process. Vitamin C helps absorb and store iron and is also an important antioxidant. Vitamin C is abundant in citrus fruits and berries, as well as in potatoes, tomatoes, peppers, cabbage, broccoli, spinach, and Brussels sprouts. The RDA is 75 mg for adult women and 90 mg for adult men.

Vitamin B1 (Thiamine) is necessary to convert food into energy: sugar becomes energy the body uses when it is mixed with Vitamin B1. Vitamin B1 has been found to help with depression[5] and diabetes.[6] B1 is critical in the production of acetylcholine, an important neurotransmitter. It is found in pork, legumes, seafood, whole grains, seeds,

---

[5] Mikkelsen K, Stojanovska L, Apostolopoulos V. The Effects of Vitamin B in Depression. Curr Med Chem. 2016;23(38):4317-4337. doi: 10.2174/0929867323666160920110810. PMID: 27655070.

[6] Thornalley PJ. The potential role of thiamine (vitamin B1) in diabetic complications. Curr Diabetes Rev. 2005 Aug;1(3):287-98. doi: 10.2174/157339905774574383. PMID: 18220605.

cauliflower, asparagus, potatoes, and kale. The RDA is 1.2 mg for males and 1.1 mg for females.

Vitamin B2 (Riboflavin) helps convert food into energy and is essential for maintaining healthy tissue. B2 has been shown to prevent migraines,[7] act as an antioxidant against some cancers,[8] [9] reduce the risk of cataracts,[10] and prevent anemia because it helps absorb iron. Foods rich in B2 include almonds, meat, dairy, eggs, salmon, legumes, spinach, and mushrooms. The RDA for adults is 1.1 mg.

Vitamin B3 (Niacin) is necessary for metabolism and nervous system function and acts as an antioxidant. It has been shown to help boost HDL (good cholesterol), which in turn reduces LDL (bad cholesterol) and ultimately lowers

---

[7] Schoenen J, Jacquy J, Lenaerts M. Effectiveness of high-dose riboflavin in migraine prophylaxis. A randomized controlled trial. Neurology. 1998 Feb;50(2):466-70. doi: 10.1212/wnl.50.2.466. PMID: 9484373.

[8] Zschäbitz S, Cheng TY, Neuhouser ML, Zheng Y, Ray RM, Miller JW, Song X, Maneval DR, Beresford SA, Lane D, Shikany JM, Ulrich CM. B vitamin intakes and incidence of colorectal cancer: results from the Women's Health Initiative Observational Study cohort. Am J Clin Nutr. 2013 Feb;97(2):332-43. doi: 10.3945/ajcn.112.034736. Epub 2012 Dec 19. PMID: 23255571; PMCID: PMC3545682.

[9] Bassett JK, Hodge AM, English DR, Baglietto L, Hopper JL, Giles GG, Severi G. Dietary intake of B vitamins and methionine and risk of lung cancer. Eur J Clin Nutr. 2012 Feb;66(2):182-7. doi: 10.1038/ejcn.2011.157. Epub 2011 Aug 31. PMID: 21878960.

[10] Skalka HW, Prchal JT. Cataracts and riboflavin deficiency. Am J Clin Nutr. 1981 May;34(5):861-3. doi: 10.1093/ajcn/34.5.861. PMID: 7234715.

total cholesterol.[11] Niacin is found in chicken, turkey, tuna, salmon, peanuts, avocados, mushrooms, peas, and potatoes. The RDA for B3 is 16 mg for men and 14 mg for women.

Vitamin B5 (Pantothenic Acid) is necessary for making blood cells, and like all the B vitamins, it helps convert food into energy. B5 promotes healthy eyes, skin, hair, and liver. It is also vital in synthesizing Coenzyme A, which is needed to create sphingosine, a lipid molecule that delivers messages inside cells. Foods rich in vitamin B5 include most meats, salmon, shellfish, grains, dairy, egg yolk, mushrooms, and vegetables such as avocado, broccoli, cauliflower, and kale. The RDA for adults is 5 mg per day.

Vitamin B6 (Pyridoxine) is necessary for brain development, nervous system stability, and a healthy immune system. It may also reduce the risk of Alzheimer's Disease.[12] Foods containing B6 include poultry, fish, chickpeas, bananas, and potatoes. The RDA for B6 after age 50 is 1.5 mg for women and 1.7 mg for men.

---

[11] Ganji SH, Kamanna VS, Kashyap ML. Niacin and cholesterol: role in cardiovascular disease (review). J Nutr Biochem. 2003 Jun;14(6):298-305. doi: 10.1016/s0955-2863(02)00284-x. PMID: 12873710.

[12] Malouf R, Grimley Evans J. The effect of vitamin B6 on cognition. Cochrane Database Syst Rev. 2003;(4):CD004393. doi: 10.1002/14651858.CD004393. PMID: 14584010.

Vitamin B7 (Biotin) helps break down macronutrients found in food into energy and regulates signals sent by cells and the activity of genes. Biotin is sometimes marketed as a treatment for hair loss and for promoting healthy hair, nails, and skin, but this is a misconception. A Biotin deficiency can cause hair loss and issues with skin and nails. But if hair loss or nail and skin issues arise from problems other than a Biotin deficiency, supplementing it has been shown to render no benefits. Food sources of B7 include beef liver, eggs, salmon, avocado, sweet potato, nuts, and seeds. There is no RDA for Biotin, but the consensus on recommended intake is 30 to 100 mcg daily.

Inositol (Vitamin B8) is not a vitamin but a sugar that helps your body process insulin. It used to be considered an essential nutrient (one that your body does not produce); however, research has shown that the liver and kidneys produce inositol from glucose, so it is no longer classified as an essential nutrient. Inositol is vital for helping your cells regulate insulin and bind neurotransmitters. It can be found in fruits, beans, grains, and nuts. There is no RDA for inositol.

Vitamin B9 (Folate) is necessary for red blood cell formation as well as healthy cell growth and function. It is also crucial in early pregnancy to reduce the risk of birth defects of the brain and spine, such as spina bifida. Folate is found in green leafy vegetables, beans, peas, nuts, citrus fruits, bananas, melons, and strawberries. Many breads and pastas now include folate as an additive with the intent to reduce birth defects. The RDA for B9 is 400 mcg per day.

Vitamin B12 (Cobalamin) is essential for red blood cell formation, cell metabolism, nerve function, and DNA production. Deficiency in B12 can cause nervous system damage. Vegans must supplement their diets with B12 as plant-based food does not produce this vitamin. Plants grown in B12-enriched soil can contain B12, but a plant does not make cobalamin. B12 is found in almost every animal product, including meats, fish, dairy, and poultry. The RDA is 2.4 mcg per day.

Water Soluble Vitamins

Vitamin	Necessity	RDA	Foods Found In
C	formation of blood vessels, cartilage, muscles & collagen necessary in healing	75 mg adult women 90 mg adult men	citrus fruits, berries potatoes, tomatoes, peppers, cabbage, broccoli, spinach and Brussel sprouts
B1	turn food to energy sugar mixes with B1 to become energy prevent depression & diabetes neurotransmitter production	1.1 mg women 1.2 mg men	pork, legumes, seafood, whole grains, seeds, kale, cauliflower, asparagus, and potatoes
B2	convert food to energy maintaining healthy tissue	1.1 mg	almonds, meat, dairy, eggs, salmon, legumes, spinach, mushrooms
B3	metabolism & nervous system antioxidant boost HDL & lower total cholesterol	14 mg women 16 mg men	chicken, turkey, tuna, salmon, peanuts, avocados, mushrooms, peas & potatoes
B5	blood cell production converts food to energy healthy eyes, skin, hair & liver synthesizing Coenzyme A	5 mg	salmon, shellfish, grains dairy, egg yolk mushrooms, avocados, broccoli, cauliflower, kale
B6	brain development nervous system stability healthy immune system may reduce Alzheimer's risk	1.5 mg women 1.7 men	poultry, fish, chickpeas, bananas & potatoes
B7	breaks down macronutrients into energy, regulates cell signals and	30-100 mcg	beef, liver, eggs, salmon, avocado, sweet potato, nuts and seeds
B8	helps body process insulin bind neurotransmitters **not a vitamin rather a sugar**	None	fruits, beans, grains and nuts
B9	red blood cell formation, healthy cell growth and function crucial in early pregnancy to prevent risk of birth defects	400 mcg	green leafy vegetables, beans, beans, peas, nuts, citrus fruits, bananas, melons & strawberries
B12	red blood cell formation, cell metabolism, nerve function and DNA production	2.4mcg	all animal products *Vegans need to supplement*

Minerals

Minerals are essential for your body, much like essential vitamins and amino acids. The word "essential" means your body cannot produce them; instead, you need to consume minerals in your diet, through either your diet or supplementation. Minerals are classified into two categories: Major minerals and trace minerals. Major minerals are used and stored in significant quantities by the body, requiring more than 100 mg/day. These include calcium, chloride, magnesium, phosphorus, potassium, sodium, and sulfur. They are important for bones, teeth, nails, nerve transmission, muscle contraction, and fluid balance. Trace minerals are also essential but are needed in smaller amounts, typically less than 100 mg daily. These include copper, chromium, cobalt, fluoride, iodine, iron, manganese, molybdenum, selenium, and zinc, which are necessary for oxygen transport, immune system function, and antioxidant defense.

Minerals are water-soluble, meaning they are best taken with a non-fat meal. It's important to use a well-stabilized preparation. For example, as mentioned earlier, calcium is best absorbed in an acidic environment. Therefore, consuming antacids as a source of calcium is not ideal, as they alter the pH of the stomach. It is important to ensure that all minerals and supplements come from high-quality, stable preparations.

Major Minerals

Potassium is found in meat, dairy, and many fruits and vegetables. The RDA is 4,700 mg, and it helps with nerve and muscle function and acts as an electrolyte. There are also indications that it may help moderate blood pressure.

Sodium is found in table salt, dairy, beets, and celery. The RDA is 2,300 mg, and it is crucial for blood pressure regulation, blood volume, and muscle and nerve function.

Calcium is found in dairy products, dark green leafy vegetables, blackstrap molasses, nuts, and some fish. Avoid using antacids as a source of calcium. The RDA is 1,000 mg, and calcium is vital for bone structure and health, nerve and muscle function, and especially cardiac function. Taking too much calcium can cause physical symptoms such as digestive issues, fatigue, muscle weakness, twitches, and bone pain. Calcium citrate is the preferred calcium compound for supplementation, as it does not neutralize stomach acid, allowing for better absorption.

Phosphorus is found in meat and dairy products. The RDA is 700 mg, and it is vital for bone formation, metabolism, and ATP production.

Magnesium is found in whole grains, nuts, and leafy green vegetables. The RDA is 310–420 mg, and it is necessary for enzyme activation, energy production, and maintaining the body's homeostatic regulation of other nutrients, such as calcium.

Chloride is found in salt, vegetables, seaweed, tomatoes, lettuce, celery, and olives. The RDA is 2,300 mg, and it is necessary for balancing bodily fluids and aiding digestion.

Sulfur is found in eggs, meats, poultry, fish, and legumes. The RDA varies depending on the source but is around 500–3,000 mg. Some sources classify sulfur as a trace mineral. Sulfur is a necessary component of amino acids.

Major Minerals			
Mineral	**Necessity**	**RDA**	**Foods Found In**
Potassium	Nerve and Muscle function electrolyte, my moderate blood pressure	4700 mg	meat, dairy, most fruits and vegetables
Sodium	Crucial for blood pressure, blood volume, muscle and nerve function	2300 mg	
Calcium	bone structure and health nerve and muscle function cardiac function	1000 mg	dairy, green leafy vegetables, backstrap, nuts some fish *Antacids are a poor source*
Phosphorus	bone formation metabolism ATP production	700 mg	meat and dairy
Magnesium	enzyme activation, energy production & regulation of other nutrients	310-420 mg	whole greens, nuts and leafy green vegetables
Chloride	balance bodily fluids digestion	2300 mg	table salt, vegetables, seaweed, tomatoes, lettuce, celery and olives
Sulfur	necessary component in	500- 3000 mg	eggs, meats, poultry, fish and legumes

Trace Minerals

Iron is found in meat, poultry, fish, shellfish, legumes, nuts, seeds, whole grains, and dark leafy green vegetables. The RDA for iron is 8–18 mg. Iron is crucial for oxygen transport in the blood and ATP production. A lack of iron can cause anemia, while too much iron can cause hemochromatosis, which can damage organs. Be cautious with iron intake: if you are not deficient, it may be best to obtain iron from your meals.

Zinc is found in meat, fish, poultry, cheese, and shellfish. The RDA is 8–11 mg. Zinc is vital for immunity, reproduction, growth, blood clotting, insulin regulation, and thyroid function.

Copper is found in seafood, organ meats, nuts, legumes, chocolate, fruits, and vegetables. The RDA is 900 mcg. Copper acts as an antioxidant and is integral to red blood cell production, nervous and immune system function, and collagen formation.

Iodine is found in fish, shellfish, garlic, lima beans, sesame seeds, soybeans, and dark leafy green vegetables. The RDA for iodine is 150 mcg, and it is important for proper thyroid function. Most table salt includes iodine as an additive. However, as people have become more conscious of blood pressure and reduced their salt intake, iodine consumption has also decreased, leading to deficiencies. Iodine deficiency can cause goiter and hypothyroidism.

Fluoride is found in water sources that are enriched by local authorities. The RDA is 3–4 mg, and fluoride is important for maintaining bone and tooth structure. Over-fluoridation during tooth development can cause fluorosis, a cosmetic condition that results in white or brown speckles on the teeth. Water fluoridation is a controversial topic due to concerns about fluoride toxicity.

Manganese is found in nuts, seeds, whole grains, and legumes. The RDA is 1.8–2.3 mg, and manganese is vital for forming connective tissue and bones, blood clotting, sex hormone development, metabolism, and brain and nerve function.

Cobalt is found in fish, nuts, leafy green vegetables, and whole grains. There is no RDA for cobalt, but the average adult intake is 5–8 mcg daily.

Selenium is found in brewer's yeast, wheat germ, liver, butter, fish, shellfish, and whole grains. The RDA is 55 mcg. Selenium is an important antioxidant and necessary for thyroid, immune system function, and brain health.

Chromium is found in whole grains, lean meats, cheese, thyme, brewer's yeast, and black pepper. The RDA is 25-35 mcg, and chromium is important for insulin function.

Molybdenum is an important enzyme cofactor found in legumes, whole grains, and nuts. The RDA for molybdenum is 45 mcg.

Trace Minerals

Mineral	Necessity	RDA	Foods Found In
Iron	oxygen transport in the blood ATP production	8 - 18 mg	neat, poultry, fish, shellfish, legumes, nuts, seeds, whole grains and green leafy vegetables
Zinc	immunity, reproduction, growth, blood clotting, insulin and thyroid function	8 -11 mg	meat, fish, poultry, cheese, shellfish
Copper	antioxidant, red blood cell production, nervous system function and collagen formation	900 ug	seafood, organ, meats, nuts, legumes, chocolate, fruits, and vegetables
Iodine	thyroid function	150 ug	fish, shellfish, garlic, lima beans, sesame seeds, soybeans, leafy green vegetables, table salt
Fluoride	maintaining bone and tooth structure	3 - 4 mg	enriched water chocolate, collared greens, pumpkin seeds, shrimp chamomile tea
Manganese	connective tissue and bone formation, blood clotting sex hormone development, metabolism, brain and nerve function	1.8 - 2.3	nuts, seeds, whole grains, and legumes
Cobalt	blood and DNA production, nerve health	No RDA avg intake: 5 - 8 mcg	fish, nuts, leafy green vegetables, whole grains
Selenium	thyroid and immune system function, brain health	55 ug	brewers yeast, whole germ, liver, butter, fish, shellfish, and whole grains
Chromium	insulin function	25 - 35 ug	whole grains, lean meats, cheese, thyme, brewer's yeast, black peppers
Molybdenum	Required for the function of four enzymes: sulfite oxidase, xanthine oxidase, aldehyde oxidase, and mitochondrial amidoxime reducing component	45 ug	legumes, whole grains, nuts

Anti-Aging and Antioxidant Supplements

As we cross over that 50-year-old threshold, our bodies may not produce the same chemicals they did when we were younger. It is important to supplement our food intake to keep our metabolism in a youthful state, which not only helps us feel better but also enables us to get the most out of our workouts, recover after pushing our bodies, and prevent free radicals and other toxic breakdowns that can occur within us. I will touch on a few critical anti-aging supplements to help you decide. Many anti-aging, brain-health, and other supplement mixtures are available in the marketplace. I decided not to review any of these because such reviews could quickly become outdated once this book is printed. Instead, I will discuss six crucial antioxidants to help you understand their benefits. Staying fit over 50 is not only about feeding ourselves and balancing our nutritional intake; it's also about understanding what happens as we age and responding accordingly.

Curcumin is the main active ingredient in turmeric. It is a potent antioxidant and may help slow the aging process. A reaction that occurs in our body, called cellular senescence,[13] means that cells stop dividing. As we age, senescence accelerates and increases the progression of aging and disease. Studies have shown that curcumin activates specific proteins, possibly delaying the senescence process.[14] Studies have also demonstrated that curcumin may combat cellular damage and delay age-related diseases.[15] Turmeric is a yellow spice frequently found in Indian cuisine but can also be taken as a supplement.

CoQ10 (Coenzyme Q10) is an antioxidant produced naturally by the body. It is necessary for energy production and protects against cellular damage. CoQ10 levels decline with age, so supplementing with it can significantly improve health and maintain youthfulness. Studies have shown that supplementing with CoQ10 can benefit heart health by increasing arterial flexibility, lowering blood pressure, and

---

[13] Lee SH, Lee JH, Lee HY, Min KJ. Sirtuin signaling in cellular senescence and aging. BMB Rep. 2019 Jan;52(1):24-34. doi: 10.5483/BMBRep.2019.52.1.290. PMID: 30526767; PMCID: PMC6386230.

[14] Bielak-Zmijewska A, Grabowska W, Ciolko A, Bojko A, Mosieniak G, Bijoch Ł, Sikora E. The Role of Curcumin in the Modulation of Ageing. Int J Mol Sci. 2019 Mar 12;20(5):1239. doi: 10.3390/ijms20051239. PMID: 30871021; PMCID: PMC6429134.

[15] Bahrami A, Montecucco F, Carbone F, Sahebkar A. Effects of Curcumin on Aging: Molecular Mechanisms and Experimental Evidence. Biomed Res Int. 2021 Oct 13;2021:8972074. doi: 10.1155/2021/8972074. PMID: 34692844; PMCID: PMC8528582.

preventing plaque buildup in your blood vessels.[16] There are also ongoing studies for those undergoing chemotherapy, showing that supplementing with CoQ10 may limit some adverse effects of chemotherapy.[17] As previously mentioned, if you are undergoing chemotherapy, consult your physician before starting any supplementation.

Quercetin is a naturally occurring pigment that belongs to a group of plant compounds known as flavonoids. It is found in some fruits, vegetables, tea, wine, and grains. Quercetin is an abundant antioxidant that helps combat free radical damage in the body. It may also reduce inflammation, allergy symptoms, and blood pressure. Research has shown that quercetin may help suppress cancers of the breast, colon, prostate, ovaries, endometrium, and lung, and may play a significant role in reducing heart disease.[18] In addition to being found in many flavonoid

---

[16] Rabanal-Ruiz Y, Llanos-González E, Alcain FJ. The Use of Coenzyme Q10 in Cardiovascular Diseases. Antioxidants (Basel). 2021 May 10;10(5):755. doi: 10.3390/antiox10050755. PMID: 34068578; PMCID: PMC8151454.

[17] Alimohammadi M, Rahimi A, Faramarzi F, Golpour M, Jafari-Shakib R, Alizadeh-Navaei R, Rafiei A. Effects of coenzyme Q10 supplementation on inflammation, angiogenesis, and oxidative stress in breast cancer patients: a systematic review and meta-analysis of randomized controlled- trials. Inflammopharmacology. 2021 Jun;29(3):579-593. doi: 10.1007/s10787-021-00817-8. Epub 2021 May 18. PMID: 34008150.

[18] Shabir Irtiqa, Kumar Pandey Vinay, Shams Rafeeya, Dar Aamir Hussain, Dash Kshirod Kumar, Khan Shafat Ahmad, Bashir Iqra,

foods; which are plant chemicals found to be high in antioxidants, anti-inflammatory and anti-cancer properties. Quercetin is also available as an over-the-counter supplement.

Nicotinamide mononucleotide (NMN) is used by several enzymes in your body to produce nicotinamide adenine dinucleotide (NADH), a water-soluble substance. NMN supplements can help improve insulin sensitivity, slow muscle aging,[19] improve heart function,[20] and reduce tiredness. NMN is naturally produced by the body, but production decreases with age. Supplementation helps counter this decline. NADH is crucial for energy metabolism, DNA repair, gene expression, and cellular

---

Jeevarathinam G., Rusu Alexandru Vasile, Esatbeyoglu Tuba, Pandiselvam R. Promising bioactive properties of quercetin for potential food applications and health benefits: A review. Frontiers in Nutrition. VOLUME=9. 2022 DOI=10.3389/fnut.2022.999752 ISSN=2296-861X

[19] de Picciotto NE, Gano LB, Johnson LC, Martens CR, Sindler AL, Mills KF, Imai S, Seals DR. Nicotinamide mononucleotide supplementation reverses vascular dysfunction and oxidative stress with aging in mice. Aging Cell. 2016 Jun;15(3):522-30. doi: 10.1111/acel.12461. Epub 2016 Mar 11. PMID: 26970090; PMCID: PMC4854911.

[20] Frederick DW, Loro E, Liu L, Davila A Jr, Chellappa K, Silverman IM, Quinn WJ 3rd, Gosai SJ, Tichy ED, Davis JG, Mourkioti F, Gregory BD, Dellinger RW, Redpath P, Migaud ME, Nakamaru-Ogiso E, Rabinowitz JD, Khurana TS, Baur JA. Loss of NAD Homeostasis Leads to Progressive and Reversible Degeneration of Skeletal Muscle. Cell Metab. 2016 Aug 9;24(2):269-82. doi: 10.1016/j.cmet.2016.07.005. PMID: 27508874; PMCID: PMC4985182.

stress response. NMN has also been shown to potentially elevate testosterone levels naturally, though more research is needed.

Resveratrol is a polyphenol chemical found in berries, certain plants, and red wine. It has strong antioxidant properties and may help prevent cancer. It is also found in blueberries, cranberries, peanuts, and grape skin. Some studies show significant benefits of resveratrol for various systems in the body.[21] These include heart and blood pressure health, as well as potential benefits for brain power and memory. Resveratrol may also reduce clotting and increase HDL levels. While it is typically recommended that resveratrol supplements be taken every other day, feel free to consume food sources of resveratrol daily.

Epigallocatechin gallate (EGCG) is a plant-based catechin compound that is part of the polyphenol group and is water-soluble. EGCG is a strong antioxidant and the primary active compound in green tea. It is also found in oolong, black, and white teas, as well as in fruits like cranberries, strawberries, blackberries, and kiwi, and in

---

[21] Weiskirchen S, Weiskirchen R. Resveratrol: How Much Wine Do You Have to Drink to Stay Healthy? Adv Nutr. 2016 Jul 15;7(4):706-18. doi: 10.3945/an.115.011627. PMID: 27422505; PMCID: PMC4942868.

foods such as cherries, peas, peaches, apples, avocados, pecans, pistachios, and hazelnuts. It is also present in dark chocolate. EGCG may help prevent heart disease and diabetes.[22] There are other supplements that claim antioxidant or anti-aging properties. I have listed just a few of the antioxidants that are well-known and documented to be effective. If you take supplements, make sure they are pure. As I have emphasized throughout this book, consult your prescribing doctor if you are undergoing treatment or taking any medication. Some supplements may interact negatively with medications, so consult your physician to avoid any problems.

---

[22] Kim HS, Quon MJ, Kim JA. New insights into the mechanisms of polyphenols beyond antioxidant properties; lessons from the green tea polyphenol, epigallocatechin 3-gallate. Redox Biol. 2014 Jan 10;2:187-95. doi: 10.1016/j.redox.2013.12.022. PMID: 24494192; PMCID: PMC3909779.

Anti-Aging and Antioxidants

Supplement	Necessity	Info
Curcumin	antioxidant may slow aging by delaying senescence	Found in Turmeric
CoQ10	antioxidant, energy production, natural levels decline with age,	supplement to make up for decreased natural levels
Quercetin	antioxidant reduces inflammation, allergy symptoms and blood pressure may reduce heart disease may suppress some cancers	found in flavonoids such as fruit, vegetables, team, wine and grains
Nicotinamide mononucleotide	produces NADH improves insulin sensitivity delay muscle aging improve heart function reduce tiredness may elevate testosterone levels	made naturally in body but decreases with age
Resveratrol	antioxidant may prevent cancer, heart and blood pressure health improve brain power and memory Reduces clotting increase HDL	found in berries, red wine blueberries, cranberries, peanuts and grape skin supplement is best taken every other day
Epigallocatechin gallate	may prevent heart disease and diabetes	active ingredient in green tea found in dark chocolate berries, kiwi, cherries peas, peaches apples, nuts, and avocados

As we age, our bodies tend not to produce the same natural chemicals they did when we were younger. Additionally, modern farming practices often strip the soil of valuable elements. Supplementing ensures you get the necessary vitamins and minerals, helping your body stay fit over 50. Slowing the aging process is not easy; it takes work, which may include supplementation. A big part of wellness is continually combating the bombardment of outside toxins on our body and mind. You may think you are eating healthy, but it is important to know the true nutritional value of your food. Be aware of whether your food is mass-produced, as this may prevent full nutrition from getting into the plant or animal. Make wise choices, which is why this chapter offers a wealth of information and a mini-encyclopedia on the vitamins, minerals, and antioxidants you should consider adding as supplements.

Chapter Five: Movement Is Life

Research has shown that a sedentary lifestyle accelerates the aging process.[1] Stagnation adversely affects your heart, increases blood pressure, causes weight gain, and increases the risk of cancer,[2] while having an overall adverse effect on your life and your health. The famous saying "Movement is life" is something our ancestors unconsciously knew long ago. People always moved their bodies; they physically worked, rested, and then repeated this process day after day. In today's age, more people live a sedentary lifestyle. A typical day for the average person includes working in a small, confined space, whether sitting or standing, bringing in lunch while forgoing movement, fresh air, and sunshine, and then spending the evening resting until bedtime. These patterns slowly repeat daily,

[1] Park JH, Moon JH, Kim HJ, Kong MH, Oh YH. Sedentary Lifestyle: Overview of Updated Evidence of Potential Health Risks. Korean J Fam Med. 2020 Nov;41(6):365-373. doi: 10.4082/kjfm.20.0165. Epub 2020 Nov 19. PMID: 33242381; PMCID: PMC7700832.

[2] Gilchrist SC, Howard VJ, Akinyemiju T, et al. Association of Sedentary Behavior With Cancer Mortality in Middle-aged and Older US Adults. JAMA Oncol. 2020;6(8):1210–1217. doi:10.1001/jamaoncol.2020.2045

aging the mind and body. When people retire, they tend to adopt these sedentary habits into their new lives.

You may be 50, 95, or any age in between. Whatever age you are, you can benefit from movement. As you read this chapter, focus on how you can apply exercise to your lifestyle. Even if you are on the older side of the "fit over 50" spectrum or suffer from an ailment, you can still benefit from movement and should keep fighting any desire to live a sedentary life. As you read this chapter, you will find various exercise options and ways to prevent injury, even if you suffer from a disability, illness, or physical challenge. This chapter introduces exercises to beginners, but those more advanced in physical fitness may also learn something new.

The chapter presents various training options you may wish to incorporate into your lifestyle. If you have not formerly been active, you will be encouraged to move your body to reverse the pattern of living in unhealthy comfort. The goal is to push yourself, move your joints, contract your muscles, utilize your total lung capacity, and get your heart pumping. All of this can be achieved; it just takes a pivot in perspective and a commitment to being healthy.

If it's been a while since you last exercised or moved your body, this book is not about judgment. We hope to reboot your mindset. Start easy; think of short-term goals with a long-term game plan and a commitment to achievement. There are a lot of "health gurus" on social media today who like to yell, call people names, and guilt them into exercising. That is not what you are going to read here. Instead, this chapter offers support and encouragement for people to begin exercising.

We will break down various sustainable methods and put you on a course to slow your aging process and reverse whatever path to ill health you may currently be on. You'll recall from the introduction the story about Joan Campbell, who took up competitive swimming at 59 years old. Regardless of your age, you can achieve it; you just need commitment.

When starting any exercise program, write down your goals and create an exercise blueprint with what you plan to achieve. Writing down your goals will keep you on track and focused. This is a way of holding yourself accountable while continuing your fitness journey without interruption. I have been working out since I was a kid, and I still have an exercise whiteboard in my workout room that allows me to stay on track and challenge myself to keep working harder.

The goals have changed, but life is about adaptation, change, and keeping fit. If exercising is new to you, or you last exercised long ago, start very slow; you are not in a race. The first few days should be a "trial and error" period to test yourself on what you can and cannot do.

Knowing the difference between "good pain" and "bad pain" is essential. Good pain is soreness from exercising, muscle fatigue, or tightness the day after. Bad pain is an injury; you should never push through an injury. During those early days, depending on what types of exercises you begin with, start at the bottom: low weights, low reps, short distances, less time, etc. In time, you will begin to find a rhythm and progress with higher and more intense levels of exercise. It's vital to always use good mechanics, as I will mention repeatedly. Injuries occur when poor mechanics are employed. I have seen and treated numerous injuries from people forfeiting good mechanics to get that last set, last mile, or extra time. Do not make that mistake. They have mirrors in gyms and health clubs, not for vanity or TikTok videos; their purpose is to allow you to watch yourself exercising and ensure you have good form. Take advantage of the mirror. If you exercise at home, get a mirror to observe.

Experiment with various exercises to identify what works best for you. There are a range of exercises, and what you start with can be something other than what you usually do. I have known people who began with calisthenics and then moved on to weight training. I have also known people who did the reverse: they didn't like weight training, so they switched to calisthenics. The point is to do what is right for you. I will say, however, that if you wish to build muscle and alter your posture and physique, you'll need to do some form of strength training.

As stated above, make sure you write down your plan. What exercises are you going to do, what days of the week, how much weight, how many reps, how many blocks, how long a run, etc., based on what you plan on doing? I always suggest that someone who has not worked out for a long time begins with some basic walking: a walk around the block, at the HS track, or even around your dining room table. Again, start slow, analyze your endurance, and build from there. After a couple of weeks, move on to whatever exercise program you wish when you find your stride. I will explain some different varieties of exercise; you can vary, mix, or do whatever feels right for you. Remember, the important thing is that you are moving, increasing your tolerance to physical activity while getting fit. Exercising can be fun, so do not consider it a chore. If exercise is not fun, something may be wrong, and you should look at what needs to be changed to make it fun.

If you get distracted or need help following through, don't exercise at home; join a gym. Accountability will keep you on track. In a gym, everyone is accountable to each other. That's not to say that you'll be counting other people's sets or reps, but the collective energy of everyone working together is palpable. You can always find someone to spot you, and if you're doing an exercise incorrectly, in a way that's not effective or could hurt you, trust me, someone will say something.

I recommend a stretch day, depending on how many days you exercise. Most forms of exercise create muscle contraction, which can leave them rigid and tighten your joints, reducing flexibility. Even if you choose yoga as your preferable exercise, I still recommend a day of restorative yoga. Besides poor mechanics, a lack of flexibility can lead to pulls, strains, and injuries. Professional football players realized this, and some, such as Lynn Swann and Herschel Walker, began practicing ballet to counter rigidity. The Dallas Cowboys even installed ballet bars outside their locker room. Regardless of your physical intensity level, stretch and remain limber. After 50, you tend to tighten up more quickly than someone younger, and you can counter this by stretching your joints and muscles at least once a week.

Strength Training

This includes free weights, machines, resistance bands, kettlebells, or anything else you use to move something heavy. There are some misconceptions about strength training. The first is the fear that by lifting weights, you will become so massive that you will look like a gorilla. I would only worry about this if you chose to train while using anabolic steroids for years. Another false belief is that you can't lose body fat from weight training. Studies have shown that weight training, or any form of strength training, increases your metabolic rate, which burns calories. Your body uses stored energy to restore and repair after your workout.[3] Weightlifting, combined with a proper diet, will also create a caloric deficit, meaning you burn more calories than you consume. (We'll break down caloric deficit later in this book.)

---

[3] LaForgia J, Withers RT, Gore CJ. Effects of exercise intensity and duration on the excess post-exercise oxygen consumption. J Sports Sci. 2006 Dec;24(12):1247-64. doi: 10.1080/02640410600552064. PMID: 17101527.

Fitness over 50 is greatly enhanced with some form of strength training. Osteoporosis, a common condition as people age, is improved by strength training.[4] A scientific principle called Wolff's Law states that bones will adapt to the loads they are required to bear. If you engage in strength training, your bones will become denser to handle the weight they constantly lift. Astronauts lose bone mass in space because there is no gravity and no force on their bones, so they need to exercise to maintain bone density. The same principle applies on Earth: pressure on the bones from exercise strengthens them.

If you want to improve your physique while becoming fit, you need to strength train. Lifting weights, resistance training, kettlebells, and other exercises will change your muscle shape and size. For example, if you're a runner, running will help you get fit, but it won't build your shoulders and arms or develop muscle hypertrophy. I know many runners who use weight training to develop musculature in ways running doesn't. The same applies to other forms of exercise that aren't classified as strength

---

[4] Hong AR, Kim SW. Effects of Resistance Exercise on Bone Health. Endocrinol Metab (Seoul). 2018 Dec;33(4):435-444. doi: 10.3803/EnM.2018.33.4.435. PMID: 30513557; PMCID: PMC6279907.

training. Keep this in mind if one of your goals is to further develop your posture and sculpt your figure.

Strength training will make you stronger, burn calories, and reduce your fall risk, which is especially important for those over 50. These exercises will improve your steadiness by adding strength to your muscles. They can lower your injury risk by improving your range of motion and mobility in your soft tissues. Strength training can also improve heart health[5] and help manage blood sugar levels. By becoming leaner, your risk of Type II diabetes decreases, and it can also help reduce the risk of some cancers.[6] Resistance training is excellent for overall health.[7]

Before starting any exercise regimen, be sure to "warm up" before and "cool down" afterward. This means stretching and performing light movements to prepare your

---

[5] Aparecida Silveira E, Vaseghi G, de Carvalho Santos AS, Kliemann N, Masoudkabir F, Noll M, Mohammadifard N, Sarrafzadegan N, de Oliveira C. Visceral Obesity and Its Shared Role in Cancer and Cardiovascular Disease: A Scoping Review of the Pathophysiology and Pharmacological Treatments. Int J Mol Sci. 2020 Nov 27;21(23):9042. doi: 10.3390/ijms21239042. PMID: 33261185; PMCID: PMC7730690.

[6] Duray M, Şimşek Ş, Yağcı N, Şenol H. The Examination of the Relationship Between Flexibility and Stability of Trunk in Older Adults. J Basic Clin Health Sci 2020; 4:140-144.

[7] Mcleod JC, Stokes T, Phillips SM. Resistance Exercise Training as a Primary Countermeasure to Age-Related Chronic Disease. Front Physiol. 2019 Jun 6;10:645. Doi: 10.3389/fphys.2019.00645. PMID: 31244666; PMCID: PMC6563593.

muscles, tendons, and joints and to mentally prepare for exercise. Don't skip this critical step. In the gym, you may see younger people start lifting without much warm-up. As we get older, our soft tissue is less flexible, so warming up and cooling down is essential for injury prevention.

Being fitter, especially through strength training, will increase your physical vigor and allow you to lift, move, and push things like never before. Strength training also stimulates your Human Growth Hormone (HGH), especially through explosive, power-based exercises. This hormone is vital for overall health.

There are many forms of strength training, and we will touch on a few. As with any exercise, make sure you start slowly. Pushing yourself to a safe level is fine; pushing yourself to injury is not. Expect to be sore for a day or two after strength training, but once you make this part of your routine, you'll embrace the soreness.

A. Weight Training

In its most basic form, weight training involves stretching, contracting, micro-tearing, and repair. Stretching and contracting with something heavy causes micro-tears in the muscle, which can be repaired with rest. During your workout, these micro-tears form, and during rest, the muscles heal. Proper strength training mechanics allow you to stretch the muscle using a specific range of motion for the joint (muscles move joints), and the weight creates these micro-tears. In the days following, these tears heal, and with repeated workouts, new micro-tears form and are repaired with new muscle tissue. This is how the muscle grows and how you can put on new muscle. The beneficial effects of weight training are that basic, along with good nutrition and proper rest.

Multiple sets and reps are performed in a controlled setting, allowing for an optimal stretch/contraction to isolate the exact muscle or muscle groups to achieve your desired results. I will stress again the importance of using good mechanics. Otherwise, you put undue stress on your joints, ligaments, tendons, and other muscles. The same goes for weights that are too heavy—stay within your ability, and over time, you can steadily increase the weight. Injuries occur quickly when mechanics are poor or when you rush your weight gains. It is common for those who put too much weight on a dumbbell or barbell to "cheat" their sets. This means using other body parts to help lift the weight. Back, elbow, and knee injuries are prevalent when cheating on reps. It is better to use lighter weights, complete a full, mechanically correct rep, avoid injury, and achieve the goal of stretch/contract/micro-tear.

A good rule is to always give yourself 72 hours before exercising a specific body part again. Rest is essential, as this is when the "repair" takes place. For example, if you work your biceps on Monday, do not exercise them again until Thursday and then not again until the following Monday. Exercising without rest puts you at risk of injury and can slow or stunt progress. If you exercise a muscle without giving it time to heal, you overwork those fibers. Most exercise physiologists recommend exercising a specific body part a maximum of twice a week. It's common to want to get back to your workout the very next day, but remember, you need the rest for repair. Use that energy to work on other body parts in the subsequent days.

Working out your upper and lower body equally will improve your overall fitness, balance your workouts, and enhance your appearance. Lower body exercises provide a more significant natural hormonal and neurological response than only exercising your upper body.[8] Your lower extremity

---

[8] Jones MT, Ambegaonkar JP, Nindl BC, Smith JA, Headley SA. Effects of unilateral and bilateral lower-body heavy resistance exercise on muscle activity and testosterone responses. J Strength Cond Res. 2012 Apr;26(4):1094-100. doi: 10.1519/JSC.0b013e318248ab3b. PMID: 22222320.

muscles are larger than those of your upper body, and because of this, they give you a more substantial response than upper body exercises. Exercising your legs also promotes increased blood flow to your lower muscles, strengthening your cardiovascular system. Lower extremity exercises improve circulation by bringing more blood to your legs and increasing the venous return of this blood to the heart. Your lower lymph nodes filter this increased lower-body circulation. As you stretch, rip, and repair your leg muscles, you are doing a great service to your overall health. Lower body exercises provide a powerful and stable foundation, improve blood flow, increase hormonal and neurological responses, and give you a more even appearance. Do not skip leg day.

There are different ways to weight train, typically using either free weights or some type of machine commonly found in most gyms. When I refer to "machine," I mean any form of exercise equipment, branded or not, that exercises you in a predetermined range of motion (e.g., Cybex, Nautilus, Smith machines). Machines offer comfort and safety, especially knowing you won't drop weights, but they also have downsides. Machines don't engage the smaller muscles or develop your proprioception.

Proprioception is your body's ability to sense the position of a body part without consciously thinking about it, including knowing where your body part (arm, leg, etc.) is without looking. Muscle tissue contains an important neurological recognition that gives your body this "proprioceptive response." While using machines, there is no proprioception awareness, as machines guide the exercise. As we age, proprioception becomes increasingly important because we tend to lose this critical neurological function, which is key to balance and steadiness, including fall prevention.

Machines don't allow for a full natural range of motion, limiting a complete muscle stretch. Not getting the full range of motion may affect the targeted muscle gains you intend to achieve. If you use machines, I suggest mixing in some free weights or resistance band exercises to help you reach your ultimate goals.

Free weights allow for a full range of motion and engage your proprioception. Unlike machine exercises, you control the entire movement, from picking up the weight, doing the set to putting the weight down. Free weights also work the stabilizer muscles and often mimic real-world competitive sports movements. The downside of free weights is that you may need a spotter for safety, and because of the free movement, you must always be conscious of your mechanics. It's easy to "cheat" with free weights, which, as mentioned earlier, can lead to injury. Cheating will prevent you from getting the intended results from your exercise. If the exercise allows and you have access, try to do each rep in front of a mirror to ensure good mechanics.

As mentioned earlier, you must be conscious of your mechanics when using free weights. You may think your form is correct, but a mirror will help confirm your movement and allow for any necessary corrective adjustments. Free weights can be more time-consuming since you have to physically change a weight plate or go get another dumbbell, whereas, with a machine, you only need to move a pin.

There are hybrids, such as cable-like exercises, which are technically machines but act more like free weights. This includes cross-cable exercises and specific pull-down exercises. These exercises allow you to control the depth and range of motion, utilizing muscle fibers that directly impact proprioceptive nerves.

The choice of how you work out is yours. Some smaller health clubs, particularly those in hotels and luxury apartment buildings, primarily have machines with a few dumbbells mixed in. Free weights give you more bang for your buck, but you can still achieve exercise, muscle growth, and fitness using machines. You can gain a lot from both categories of equipment by identifying your goals, adapting your exercise program, and paying attention to mechanics. Both types of equipment offer benefits.

Range of motion (ROM) is significant in reaching your weightlifting goals. Many find that dumbbell exercises are the best way to improve ROM, as they allow for a better muscle stretch than barbell exercises. Both are excellent for weight training but should be used with different goals in mind. A barbell allows for more power moves, such as bench presses, squats, or deadlifts. Dumbbells, because they are moved independently, offer more freedom with respect to range of movement.

Dumbbell

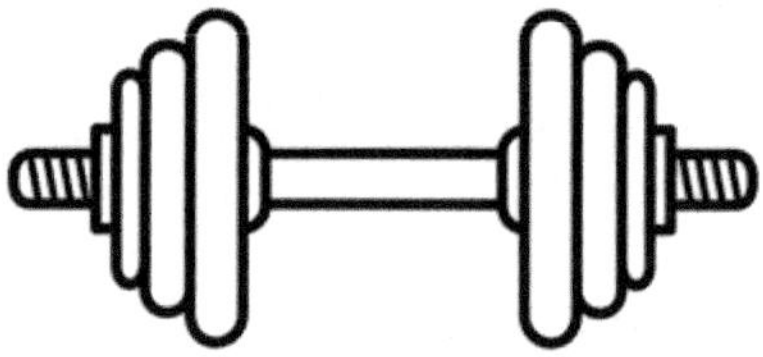

Dumbbells may be used for an entire upper-body workout, including the previously mentioned bench press, while some feel that barbells are best for lower-body exercises. Due to their independence and freedom of movement, dumbbells are also excellent for correcting muscle imbalances, whether due to strength, conditioning, or rehabilitation, while allowing you to sculpt your muscles. Barbells, on the other hand, are very effective for lower-body and core exercises.

Barbell

Kettlebells are another type of weight that allows for multi-joint movement, which makes them very efficient for your training. Both dumbbell and barbell training are primarily single-joint exercises, meaning they focus on stretch and contraction. Kettlebells, however, offer even more range of motion, simulating more "real-life" actions. Kettlebell exercises put your body through more natural movements than the isolation provided by dumbbells and barbells. As with the other two options, proper mechanics are essential, and when swinging the kettlebell, you need to ensure you're doing so in a clear and specific pattern.

Kettlebell

All three forms of weight training have their advantages, and there are no real downsides unless you fail to warm up, use poor mechanics, or neglect to complement your fitness routine with a good diet.

An essential aspect of weight training is exercise splits, which allow you to work muscles whose actions are similar and benefit one another. Splits refer to exercises performed on the same day. For example, exercising the triceps and shoulders on the same day as the chest will help complement each muscle's development. The same applies to working your back: you could add biceps, shoulders, legs, calves, and abdominal muscles on the same day. These exercises share similar actions and will benefit one another. Strong triceps and shoulders will help you push more weight when bench pressing, just as strong calves will assist with squatting.

When putting together your workout schedule, assign exercise splits that support each other.

Another option is to join weightlifting group classes, where a trainer directs a group through circuit training, kickboxing, or other exercise routines. Classes are a great way to stay accountable and have the supervision of someone knowledgeable about proper mechanics and safety. As I've mentioned throughout this book, study and talk with others, but make sure you know what you're doing before you ever get under the bar.

Resistance bands are another form of strength training that falls under the weight training category. These rubber strips provide resistance during workouts, mimicking the action of weight training by placing a load on your muscles. Resistance bands come in various strengths and can be used for push or pull exercises. You can attach the band to an inanimate object, such as a door, or hold it down with a body part to create a stretch–contractional action. One of the practical benefits of resistance bands is that they are much less expensive and require minimal storage space. They are excellent for those with physical limitations but are suitable for anyone at any age, whether as a complement to other exercises or as a primary fitness tool.

B. Calisthenics

If you don't have access to weights or are not interested in weight training, you can always use your body weight. Calisthenics, which were part of high school gym class for many, can work almost all your muscles. Examples include push-ups, planks, body squats, lunges, and exercises with a bar, such as pull-ups, dips, and rows. There are numerous variations of calisthenics, and changing the angle of an exercise can target a different part of the muscle or even a completely different muscle group.

Bodyweight exercises allow you to stretch and contract every skeletal muscle, and they cost nothing while being highly effective. Don't overlook bodyweight exercises as a viable option for strength training. All you need is a small space, a set plan, and the motivation to push yourself.

C. Aerobic and Anaerobic Exercise

Aerobic exercise involves performing intense movements where your heart rate increases and oxygen is the primary source of energy. Aerobic exercise contrasts with anaerobic exercise, which also elevates your heart rate but uses different forms of respiration. Let me explain: Anaerobic exercise uses glucose stored in your muscles for energy, while aerobic exercise breaks down stored glucose, fats, and oxygen for energy. Anaerobic exercises are typically fast, short bursts of activity, while aerobic exercises are longer in duration. Some exercises, like CrossFit, incorporate both aerobic and anaerobic elements.

Aerobic exercises include running, jogging, swimming, and "aerobic classes"—extended forms of exercise designed to make you sweat, breathe heavily, and burn calories. During aerobic exercise, pay attention to your breathing: once you start panting, you've transitioned from aerobic to anaerobic respiration. When this happens, it's best to slow down your activity until you catch your breath and then pick up again. For example, reduce running to a jog or walk, or if swimming, slow down from full speed to a slower glide. In an aerobic class, if you begin panting, switch to walking in place. This will help keep you in aerobic respiration mode.

Some benefits of aerobic exercise include increased stamina, improved cardiovascular health, decreased risk of chronic illness, and maintaining a healthy weight. Aerobic exercises have always been around, often used in training for sports, typically in the form of running. Whether it be laps, sprints, biking, or long jogs, aerobics has always played a part in "getting in shape." Recently, sports physiology has recognized that you can blend different types of aerobic exercises.

If you are new to aerobic exercise or haven't participated in a while, start at your own pace. Becoming fit doesn't mean starting at a point that leaves you injured or discouraged. I recommend beginning slowly. If you want to run, start by walking. If it's swimming, do a couple of laps. If you want to join a class, start with the beginners. Over time, your body will tell you when it's ready to pick up the pace.

As with all exercises, ensure you have the proper equipment, including good sneakers. Your shoes should be designed for the exercise you will perform and not worn out. I have treated injuries from people training with old, uneven sneakers.

Anaerobic exercises are high-intensity movements performed in short bursts. The most popular form is HIIT (high-intensity interval training). The intent is to push yourself hard for a specific amount of time. Examples include battle ropes, sprints, burpees, jumping rope, and circuit training. During these exercises, your body quickly builds up lactic acid, which is formed when your body uses carbohydrates for energy. Your liver and kidneys then break down the lactic acid to create new glucose molecules.

Anaerobic exercises offer the same health benefits as aerobic exercises but use a different physiological pathway to achieve them. They can also increase strength, promote weight loss, and improve endurance.

When training after age 50, paying attention to your cardiovascular health and the environment in which you train is essential. Cold weather constricts blood flow, putting pressure on your heart and arteries. If you suffer from high blood pressure or any potential heart condition, be mindful of the effects cold weather may have on your body during exercise.

Always ensure you are hydrated. Hydration is often neglected when exercising in the cold or water. Your muscles can cramp, and you could become dehydrated. I see this when swimming; you may not feel noticeably sweaty or hot, but your body still loses water during training. Do not neglect hydration.

Aerobic training can create an enormous calorie deficit when performed at high levels. Marathon runners are an example of this. If your goal is to lose weight, aerobic exercise can help achieve that. However, if your goal is to maintain weight, you may face unintended consequences. Once your body exhausts all its circulating glucose and fat stores, it will begin to break down muscle for energy. It is important to know your caloric intake and output. Make sure you fuel up and drink water to maintain your desired weight.

Playing sports is also a great way to engage in aerobic or anaerobic exercise. Activities like tennis, basketball, handball, pickleball, or biking provide a great workout. These sports allow you to burn calories while having fun. Believe it or not, you can burn a significant number of calories playing a round of golf. Although golf may seem laid-back, the walking involved can burn 1,500 to 2,000 calories per round, depending on the terrain and the weight of your golf bag.

D. Yoga

Yoga checks all the boxes for improving flexibility, strength, tone, and endurance. The most obvious and notable benefit is flexibility. The various poses and how they are performed are excellent for improving flexibility. As discussed earlier, maintaining flexibility helps prevent injury. By including yoga in any exercise program, you will enhance your overall flexibility and reduce the risk of potential injuries.

Many people don't realize that yoga can also increase strength and tone. Yoga poses require you to hold sustained contractions in multiple muscle groups, using your body weight to build lean muscle. Combined with a healthy diet, practicing yoga alone can lead to a lean, muscular physique while promoting overall fitness.

Yoga also improves endurance in several ways. It focuses on concentration, mechanics, and breathing. Yoga enhances your range of motion with greater flexibility, improves your stride and joint movement, and lengthens your muscles. These benefits help you move more freely, prevent injury, and slow the aging process. By improving concentration and breathing efficiency, yoga enhances oxygen usage, supporting both aerobic and anaerobic activities and allowing you to build greater endurance. Yoga is also a challenging workout in itself. Completing a session in a relaxed, focused way improves lung capacity and overall exercise tolerance.

I am also a proponent of restorative yoga. As the name suggests, it helps your body recover and restore itself. It is an excellent way to relieve stress, aid injury recovery, and recuperate from other workouts. This brings us to the next topic.

E. Alternatives

What if you have lumbar stenosis, a disability, or limitations in your range of motion? If you suffer from a condition that severely restricts your ability to perform floor exercises, weightlifting, or other activities I've discussed, you can and should still exercise. Alternatives such as chair yoga, pool aerobics, adaptive cardio exercises, and other movements allow you to move through whatever condition you may be experiencing.

I want you to be fit regardless of age or history. If you picked up this book at 91 years old and have rarely exercised, you can still do something appropriate for your age and fitness level. Over the years, I've had many patients, some younger and some older, with severely limited physical abilities for various reasons. You can still perform movements in a controlled, safe environment, whether with a personal trainer, in a group class, or just by following a video. Each of these options will provide a good workout. Exercise is accessible to anyone and everyone who wishes to do it. Don't get frustrated if I mention squats or other specific exercises you cannot perform. Start at your current physical level; this isn't a competition. Your goal is to become as fit as possible, given your own specific situation.

And as we emphasized earlier, it should be enjoyable; if not, you're not doing it right.

F. Stretching on Off Days

I briefly touched on this earlier, but stretching is important to include in your exercise program. I always suggest having a stretching day, preferably on one of your "off days." Most exercises, excluding yoga, can tighten your musculoskeletal system. If left that way, your body may become less flexible and form adhesions. The days of the hypertonic, immobile weightlifter are long gone. Today, athletes are encouraged to stretch to counter the unintended negative effects of regular training.

One of the biggest hindrances to "remaining young" is flexibility, or the lack of it. Of all the components necessary to stay fit, flexibility ranks near the top. Maintaining good flexibility benefits your muscles and joints and improves circulation. Remaining flexible or improving your flexibility will support and enhance any other exercises you do. A study published in the Journal of Clinical Health Science concluded, "Loss of flexibility is a more important risk factor than aging for balance and stability impairment. It is suggested that treatment protocols should include approaches that increase body flexibility aimed at increasing body stability." Think of exercise as part of a complete program. Don't focus only on your specific workout; think about your diet, breathing, mechanics, stretching, and your overall fitness program.

There is a difference between the stretching you do before or after your workout and a dedicated stretching program. The first is meant to warm up your muscles and allow your joints to move through their range of motion to prepare for your exercise session or cool down afterward. The latter is a session dedicated to elongating your muscles, preventing stiffness, and breaking up adhesions, which improves your range of motion, overall health, and prevents injury.

A stretching program doesn't need to be as long as your workout session; 15–30 minutes is sufficient. You only need enough time to go through a series of motions to counteract the tightness in exercised muscles and joints, restore their flexibility, and elongate them. You can follow various stretching programs or participate in a restorative yoga class. Whatever you choose, make it part of your weekly routine to prevent the tightness, stiffness, and muscle imbalances that come from being inflexible.

Active vs. Passive Stretching

There are two highly effective yet different forms of stretching: active and passive. Active stretching involves elongating a muscle and moving a joint by contracting other muscles. You're using your strength to stretch your muscles. The benefit of active stretching is that you can control the depth of the stretch, which helps prevent overstretching or injury.

Passive stretching, including Proprioceptive Neuromuscular Facilitation (PNF), involves resting your body while an external force moves your body part. This force could be a strap, your body weight, or someone else helping to stretch you. The significant benefit of passive stretching is that your body part can be moved further than you could stretch it actively, creating a better range of motion.

G. Dynamic vs. Static Stretching to Warm-Up

As mentioned earlier, warming up is something you do before your exercise program. It helps prepare your muscles, joints, and tendons for your training session, breaking up small adhesions, getting your blood pumping, and readying your body for the task ahead. There are two types of warm-up stretches: static and dynamic.

Static stretching is done in place, either standing or sitting. Examples include stretching your pectoralis on a door frame, bending over to warm up your back, or sitting while doing a hurdler's stretch. Static stretches help lengthen your muscles and prepare your joints for activities that require flexibility.[9]

Dynamic stretching involves actively moving your whole body. If you arrive early for a college or professional game, you might see athletes performing jumping jacks, hip openers, or crossover/karaoke stretches. Dynamic stretching is more specific to certain activities and is the preferred method for those who will be running, jumping, or working out.[10,11]

In this chapter, you were briefly introduced to various exercises you can try. Finding the right one is a personal choice; the key is to do something that suits you and your

---

[9] Page P. Current concepts in muscle stretching for exercise and rehabilitation. Int J Sports Phys Ther. 2012 Feb;7(1):109-19. PMID: 22319684; PMCID: PMC3273886.

[10] Opplert J, Babault N. Acute Effects of Dynamic Stretching on Muscle Flexibility and Performance: An Analysis of the Current Literature. Sports Med. 2018 Feb;48(2):299-325. doi: 10.1007/s40279-017-0797-9. PMID: 29063454.

[11] Zmijewski P, Lipinska P, Czajkowska A, Mróz A, Kapuściński P, Mazurek K. Acute Effects of a Static Vs. a Dynamic Stretching Warm-up on Repeated-Sprint Performance in Female Handball Players. J Hum Kinet. 2020 Mar 31;72:161-172. doi: 10.2478/hukin-2019-0043. PMID: 32269657; PMCID: PMC7126248.

goals rather than simply following the crowd. If you're new to exercise or haven't done it in a long time, start easy. There's no need to push yourself too hard or too quickly. The most important thing is to prevent injuries or other health issues, as negative outcomes often occur when you don't follow proper mechanics or work at a pace that isn't right for you.

Science is continuously learning more and more about the importance of exercise and maintaining healthy, strong muscle tissue. A recent study showed that "muscle mass could be an important new prognostic factor for survival and treatment tolerability in cancer patients."[12] Obesity, especially as we age, has been demonstrated to be a risk factor for cancer.

Throughout this chapter, I emphasize the importance of proper mechanics, but all forms of safety are significant. I've mentioned it before, but if you don't know what you're doing, consult someone who does. You can work with a personal trainer or a training buddy who has exercise knowledge. The fitness world has some great people; you

---

[12] Rier HN, Jager A, Sleijfer S, Maier AB, Levin MD. The Prevalence and Prognostic Value of Low Muscle Mass in Cancer Patients: A Review of the Literature. Oncologist. 2016 Nov;21(11):1396-1409. doi: 10.1634/theoncologist.2016-0066. Epub 2016 Jul 13. PMID: 27412391; PMCID: PMC5189631.

just need to ask for help. Don't stop learning. Read books on exercise, watch videos, and become a student of your fitness—own it! The fact that you are taking this journey to become fit over 50, 60, 70, and beyond is an important first step. Now you must act on it and incorporate exercise into your life, because fitness over 50 means understanding that movement is life.

Chapter Six: Keep Talking, Keep Communicating with Others and Keep Your Mind Stimulated

As you move through your 50th birthday, your mind is likely as sharp as ever, but things may change as you reach your 60s, 70s, and 80s. Your eyesight might weaken, your hearing may decline, and your thought process may not remain as sharp as when you were younger. Our goal in staying fit over 50 is to delay these changes. Staying fit includes keeping your mind sharp, focused, and full of active, positive thoughts. Surrendering to father time should not be an option. I am not talking about neurological diseases such as Alzheimer's or dementia but about keeping your everyday thinking precise and quick. Let's focus on staying fit in mind and body.

Nobody wants to suffer from increased confusion or disorientation as they age. We all want to be robust, mentally sharp middle-aged or older individuals who can remember, think on their feet and respond quickly. Brain wellness is essential for overall fitness; without it, everything else fails.

Eating right and having a great exercise routine will benefit your mind, as research has proven,[1,2] but to keep it razor sharp, you must put your brain to work. It's not difficult, but you must make time for it and commit, just like with physical fitness.

Staying Social

One of the key topics in anti-aging is staying social. You don't need to surround yourself with many people, and you certainly don't want to be around toxic people. The idea is to be social with people who engage you, make you think, and stimulate you intellectually. Studies reinforce the idea that maintaining social relationships throughout your life helps keep your mind sharp as you age.[3] Similar studies have shown that living an isolated lifestyle can lead to a significant decline in mental acuity, dementia, depression,

---

[1] Devore EE, Kang JH, Breteler MM, Grodstein F. Dietary intakes of berries and flavonoids in relation to cognitive decline. Ann Neurol. 2012 Jul;72(1):135-43. doi: 10.1002/ana.23594. Epub 2012 Apr 26. PMID: 22535616; PMCID: PMC3582325.

[2] Grodstein, Francine & Kang, Jae & Glynn, Robert & Cook, Nancy & Gaziano, J. (2007). A Randomized Trial of Beta Carotene Supplementation and Cognitive Function in Men: The Physicians' Health Study II. Archives of internal medicine. 167. 2184-90. 10.1001/archinte.167.20.2184.

[3] Julianne Holt-Lunstad, Timothy B Smith, J. Bradley Layton. Social Relationships and Mortality Risk: A Meta-analytic Review. PLOS Medicine. July 27, 2010

and chronic illness.[4] Isolation can create feelings of loneliness and disconnection from the world.

As we move through life, we make friends, lose friends, and make more friends—the cycle continues. This pattern is part of life, though it doesn't mean you lose every friend you've ever made. In the big picture, throughout a lifetime, you won't always associate with the same tribe. It's essential to continue forming relationships and having someone with whom you can talk, enhancing your mental sharpness.

This book is about fitness, and a big part of that is physical exercise, which is the longest chapter. Working out not only helps your body but also helps retain your mental edge, especially as you age.[5] You can also use this opportunity to be social. In the gym, there are plenty of people to connect with, talk to, and be around. I mentioned

---

[4] National Academies of Sciences, Engineering, and Medicine; Division of Behavioral and Social Sciences and Education; Health and Medicine Division; Board on Behavioral, Cognitive, and Sensory Sciences; Board on Health Sciences Policy; Committee on the Health and Medical Dimensions of Social Isolation and Loneliness in Older Adults. Social Isolation and Loneliness in Older Adults: Opportunities for the Health Care System. Washington (DC): National Academies Press (US); 2020 Feb 27. 3, Health Impacts of Social Isolation and Loneliness on Morbidity and Quality of Life.

[5] Babaei P, Azari HB. Exercise Training Improves Memory Performance in Older Adults: A Narrative Review of Evidence and Possible Mechanisms. Front Hum Neurosci. 2022 Jan 27;15:771553. doi: 10.3389/fnhum.2021.771553. PMID: 35153701; PMCID: PMC8829997.

earlier people like Jim, whom I met at the gym. You don't have to become best friends with everyone you work out with, but you can strike up conversations. You're in a space where everyone shares a common interest: exercise. You can offer to spot someone, ask about a particular exercise, discuss fitness goals, or even talk about this book. Exercise classes are a fantastic way to be social, too. Everyone is working out together and experiencing the same process, and everyone should have a good endorphin rush afterward. A gym is a built-in space to meet and converse with people, so take advantage of it, especially if you're looking to make new connections.

It's important to associate with people who share your interests and values. The gym is one example of a place where your interests intersect. As a bonus, connecting with people during exercise can increase accountability and boost your workout results. There are many other ways to meet people and be social. Stepping out of your comfort zone and testing the waters is crucial. You may find that others are just as eager to form social connections.

If you're interested in politics, history, or other topics, join a group that aligns with your interests. Libraries, places of worship, American Legion halls, and many other places often hold seminars and discussions that may appeal to you.

These are excellent opportunities to be around people and strike up conversations.

If you're hesitant to talk with strangers, keep your goals small. Don't walk into a crowded room and think you have to engage with everyone. That can be intimidating and overwhelming, a common reason people fear crowds. Remember, you don't need to interact with the whole room. Start small by finding one person or a small group to talk to. If you have your social antenna up, you can tell who is inviting and who is not. In these social settings, people are usually interested in meeting others but work small. It is much easier to size up a crowd and find one or two people to start or join a conversation. Look for someone who may not know anyone else, either. They will be open for discussion right away.

This same approach applies to the gym. Don't feel like you have to engage with the entire room. Find someone at your fitness level and offer a spot, or ask for one. While this book isn't about making friends, these tips may help you open doors and connect with others.

Other Social Structures

If you are fortunate, you may have a built-in support system right around you—your family. Studies have shown that maintaining communication with family improves well-being as we age.[6] Keeping family relationships and conversations alive is highly social. Engaging in discussions, visiting or watching a ball game together, and spending time in the kitchen can help keep your mind active, engaged, and youthful. Intergenerational family communication keeps your mind alive on many levels. Ties with siblings, younger grandchildren, nephews, nieces, and, if you're lucky, older family members are priceless. Being fit over 50 and addressing the social aspect of life is incredibly beneficial for nurturing these relationships.

I've also found it helpful to be in a social environment that promotes a youthful mentality. Being around younger people can help keep you youthful. If you live near a college, visit the campus, watch games, attend theater productions, or sit in on lectures. Volunteer at the school and immerse yourself in the activities of youth. Nothing feels more youthful than being around energetic kids. Visit the campus libraries to read your books, articles, or newspapers. You don't have to engage with students, but simply being in that environment can help keep you spry. Think about the energy

---

[6] Patricia A Thomas, Hui Liu, Debra Umberson, Family Relationships and Well-Being, Innovation in Aging, Volume 1, Issue 3, November 2017, igx025,

of attending a college sporting event. There are three sports seasons a year, and not everyone at these games is young: there are alumni, parents, and other fans. It doesn't have to be a big school either; most Division 3 schools have nice fields, plenty of bleachers, and a variety of sports each season. Root for the teams and enjoy the excitement of youth.

The same goes for attending college arts performances, band competitions, and other events. Be a part of the younger generation's journey as they strive for success in their endeavors. Attending these events can help keep your mind youthful. Studies have shown that being around youth helps you stay young.[7] Take advantage of these opportunities that may be around you—all you have to do is look for them. Don't feel intimidated by crowds when attending events. Find a friendly area to sit or stand and enjoy. Every town or neighboring town has a high school with performances you can attend. Volunteering at events can be a useful way of making connections.

---

[7] Anna Krzeczkowska, David M. Spalding, William J. McGeown, Alan J. Gow, Michelle C. Carlson, Louise A. Brown Nicholls, A systematic review of the impacts of intergenerational engagement on older adults' cognitive, social, and health outcomes, Ageing Research Reviews, Volume 71, 2021, 101400, ISSN 1568-1637

As we say to kids, the same applies to older adults: avoid getting stuck on your computer. There is nothing truly social there, even if they call it "social media." It can give you tunnel vision and lead to living in isolation on your phone or computer. While these devices are great tools, they shouldn't replace your social life. Nothing beats human interaction. Charles Ashworth wrote,

> "It is imperative for our mental health to have a true connection with other humans, intimate conversations with eye contact and touch, an empathetic heart in the presence of others, and open ears when asking someone about their well-being both in and out of their professional lives. Digital connection should never be an alternative to the natural interactions of human beings."[8]

Human connection is essential for keeping your mind young, sharp, and fit. While eating right and exercising benefit the brain, social connections are vital.

This chapter and the next focus on keeping your mind sharp and your memory strong. As we age, some things slip away from us, possibly because the world is constantly

---

[8] Charles Ashworth, Are We Losing the Human Connection? Forbes Magazine August 1, 2019

changing. The days of the Sony Walkman, 8-track tapes, and cable TV are behind us, with newer technologies emerging every day. Our world has evolved, and our difficulty in immediately grasping this newness can earn us labels like the "Keep the remote away from Grandpa/Grandma" generation. Besides following the plans in these chapters, keep yourself updated on the latest technology, innovations, and ideas. Learning how to use computer updates can stimulate your mind. You don't need to immerse yourself in pop culture, but staying aware of modern gadgets will keep you thinking and your neurons firing. Never let your circuits get old; keep talking and stimulating your mind.

Chapter Seven: Eating for a Sharp Mind

We will revisit food selections, but this time, we will focus on how your eating habits can sharpen your mind or, conversely, how poor dietary choices can adversely affect your mental capacity. Various foods and supplements may positively impact mental acuity. When discussing supplements that help the brain, we refer to natural formulations of beneficial chemicals found in foods. Remember, supplements are meant to "supplement" your eating habits, not replace them. Your body is an engine that functions at its best when fueled correctly. When fueled improperly, you hinder its full genetic potential, preventing you from being as fit as possible.

Think of it this way: when you eat something unhealthy, your body must expend significant energy combating the harmful ingredients and toxins, whether those elements lead to high blood pressure, a weakened immune system, or cognitive decline. Your immune system, liver, and other organs divert valuable energy to eliminate these harmful agents. Healthier food choices, on the other hand, allow your body to focus on building positively, keeping you physically, emotionally, and mentally strong. Since you want to be fit over 50, doesn't it make sense to make choices that benefit rather than break down your body? Your brain is an organ that needs to be nourished, filled with positive thoughts, kept socially engaged, and exercised regularly. Studies show that diet plays a role in preventing cognitive decline.[1] The choice is yours; make the right decisions and stay sharp.

The Negative Effects of Sugar on the Brain

Your brain needs sugar to survive. Glucose is the primary source of energy for the brain, which uses about half of the body's total energy supply. In earlier chapters, we discussed different types of sugars, such as glucose and fructose, found in nature and essential for brain function. There are exceptions, particularly when someone follows a healthy ketogenic diet, where the brain uses ketone bodies as an alternative energy source. This only happens with a properly executed keto plan.

But what happens when you consume high levels of sugar from processed foods and desserts? Natural sugars in

---

[1] Dominguez LJ, Barbagallo M. Nutritional prevention of cognitive decline and dementia. Acta Biomed. 2018 Jun 7;89(2):276-290. doi: 10.23750/abm.v89i2.7401. PMID: 29957766; PMCID: PMC6179018.

fruits and vegetables come with fiber, which helps prevent overindulgence. Processed foods, however, often lack fiber and are loaded with sucrose, leading to an unhealthy surge of sugar in your body and brain. Studies show that high levels of glucose intake can impair cognitive function and increase the risk of dementia.[2,3] High-sugar diets have been shown to affect memory, particularly in the hippocampus. A 2015 study demonstrated how high sucrose levels can lead to memory deficits.[4]

Sugar causes the hippocampus to reduce the number of new memory cells and triggers the release of inflammatory chemicals. Sugar also affects the mesolimbic dopamine system of the brain. This is the area that releases the hormone dopamine whenever it is stimulated. Dopamine is the

---

[2] Samaras K, Lutgers HL, Kochan NA, Crawford JD, Campbell LV, Wen W, Slavin MJ, Baune BT, Lipnicki DM, Brodaty H, Trollor JN, Sachdev PS. The impact of glucose disorders on cognition and brain volumes in the elderly: the Sydney Memory and Ageing Study. Age (Dordr). 2014 Apr;36(2):977-93. doi: 10.1007/s11357-013-9613-0. Epub 2014 Jan 9. PMID: 24402401; PMCID: PMC4039246

[3] Gillespie KM, White MJ, Kemps E, Moore H, Dymond A, Bartlett SE. The Impact of Free and Added Sugars on Cognitive Function: A Systematic Review and Meta-Analysis. Nutrients. 2023 Dec 25;16(1):75. doi: 10.3390/nu16010075. PMID: 38201905; PMCID: PMC10780393.

[4] Reichelt AC, Killcross S, Hambly LD, Morris MJ, Westbrook RF. Impact of adolescent sucrose access on cognitive control, recognition memory, and parvalbumin immunoreactivity. Learn Mem. 2015 Mar 16;22(4):215-24. doi: 10.1101/lm.038000.114. PMID: 25776039; PMCID: PMC4371171.

"reward chemical" and often the culprit for addictive behavior. The release of this hormone makes the brain believe it is being rewarded, similar to when someone uses illicit drugs. This addictive-like cycle can rewire the brain into a situation where you crave excess sugar even though it has a deleterious effect on the brain. If you have lived most of your life with a high-sugar diet, your brain is most likely wired to need to be rewarded with something sweet to feel satisfied.

Recognizing a sugar addiction and developing a plan to reduce sugar intake is crucial. Understanding why you constantly crave sugar can help you break the cycle. This book is about real-life strategies for being fit over 50. It's unrealistic to think most people won't enjoy a dessert now and then. The key is to avoid overindulgence and resist the urge to make processed sugar a regular part of your diet. Being fit is a choice and a commitment, and this is one area where staying committed to fighting the impulse is vital to long-term success.

Bad Fats and the Brain

Fat is essential for the brain, but just like with sugar, choosing the right types of fat is crucial. A 2012 study found that "A dietary pattern with relatively high caloric intake from carbohydrates and low caloric intake from fat and proteins may increase the risk of mild cognitive impairment or dementia in elderly persons."[5]As discussed in an earlier chapter, we know that fats are necessary for brain function, but the wrong fats can be harmful. A 2004 study found that prospective dietary studies conducted in Chicago,[6] New York,[7] and Rotterdam[8] also examined the relation of dietary fat intake to the development of Alzheimer's disease. The Chicago study reported the strongest evidence of an association. High intake of saturated fat doubled the risk of Alzheimer's disease, and even moderate intake of trans fat increased the risk by 2 to 3 times. By contrast, a higher intake of both polyunsaturated and monounsaturated fats was

---

[5] Roberts RO, Roberts LA, Geda YE, Cha RH, Pankratz VS, O'Connor HM, Knopman DS, Petersen RC. Relative intake of macronutrients impacts risk of mild cognitive impairment or dementia. J Alzheimers Dis. 2012;32(2):329-39. doi: 10.3233/JAD-2012-120862. PMID: 22810099; PMCID: PMC3494735.

[6] Morris MC, Evans DA, Bienias JL, et al. Dietary fats and the risk of incident Alzheimer's disease. Arch Neurol. 2003;60:194–200. Abstract.

[7] Luchsinger JA, Min-Xing T, Shea S, Mayeux R. Caloric intake and the risk of Alzheimer disease. Arch Neurol. 2002;59:1258–1263

[8] Kalmijn S, Launer LJ, Ott A, Witteman JC, Hofman A, Breteler MM. Dietary fat intake and the risk of incident dementia in the Rotterdam Study. Ann Neurol. 1997;42:776–782

associated with a lower risk of developing Alzheimer's disease.[9]

It cannot be stressed enough: healthy fats are important for brain health, but the key word is healthy.

High levels of saturated and trans fats have been linked to poor cognitive function. Previously, we discussed how these fats negatively affect heart health, and now we see their detrimental effects on the brain. A 2012 study found that those on a high saturated-fat diet had decreasing cognitive function and verbal memory, whereas those who consumed mostly monounsaturated fats showed improved memory.[10]

There are numerous studies highlighting the harmful effects of trans fats on the brain. This type of fat is artificial and primarily used by companies to process foods more cheaply. A 2015 study showed that the consumption of trans fats dramatically decreases memory in adults under 45.[11]

---

[9] Morris MC. Diet and Alzheimer's disease: what the evidence shows. MedGenMed. 2004 Jan 15;6(1):48. PMID: 15208559; PMCID: PMC114070

[10] Okereke OI, Rosner BA, Kim DH, Kang JH, Cook NR, Manson JE, Buring JE, Willett WC, Grodstein F. Dietary fat types and 4-year cognitive change in community-dwelling older women. Ann Neurol. 2012 Jul;72(1):124-34. doi: 10.1002/ana.23593. Epub 2012 May 18. Erratum in: Ann Neurol. 2012 Oct;72(4):627. PMID: 22605573; PMCID: PMC3405188.

[11] Golomb BA, Bui AK. A Fat to Forget: Trans Fat Consumption and Memory. PLoS One. 2015 Jun 17;10(6):e0128129. doi:

Trans fats increase oxidative stress, which is an imbalance between free radicals and antioxidants. Antioxidants neutralize free radicals, but with a diet high in trans fats, you introduce more free radicals and fewer antioxidants into your system. Trans fats also increase inflammation, interfere with lipid metabolism, and disrupt brain lipid production. Given that the brain is composed of 60% fat, this interference is detrimental to brain impulse transmission.

Study subjects who consumed a diet high in monounsaturated fats, such as those found in the Mediterranean Diet, showed improved learning, slower cognitive decline, and a reduced risk of Alzheimer's disease. Moreover, the monounsaturated diet increased the production of acetylcholine, a neurotransmitter vital for learning and memory. When acetylcholine levels decrease, memory issues can arise, as seen in Alzheimer's disease. Monounsaturated diets help boost acetylcholine production.

Another fat that benefits the brain is Omega-3 fatty acids. Sixty percent of your brain is made up of fat, and 50% of that fat consists of Omega-3 fatty acids. These fatty acids have been shown to improve neuron structure, enhance

---

10.1371/journal.pone.0128129. PMID: 26083739; PMCID: PMC4470692.

cognitive function, and reduce cognitive decline. Later in this chapter, we will discuss where Omega-3s can be found.

Seed oils, which have now replaced trans fats as a cheap and convenient cooking oil, have been shown to increase chronic inflammation due to their high levels of Omega-6 fatty acids. Ideally, there should be a 1:1 ratio of Omega-3s to Omega-6s in the diet. Seed oils can disrupt this balance, diminishing the benefits of Omega-3 fatty acids.

Good Things to Eat

Our goal is to be fit over 50, 60, 70, and beyond. Feed your brain in ways that support this vital organ. Add some of these foods to your diet if you haven't already. As discussed earlier, much of today's food supply has been stripped of nutrients due to modern agricultural practices. Consider supplementing your food intake where necessary. Remember, supplements are meant to supplement your diet, not replace it. Eating brain-healthy foods and supplementing wisely can make the difference between health and wellness or disease and decline. Here are some foods to consider adding to your diet. You don't need to eat all of them, but incorporating some can make a noticeable difference:

Green Leafy Vegetables: Spinach, collards, kale, and broccoli are high in calcium and also contain Vitamin K, folate, beta-carotene, lutein, and antioxidants. Lutein and folate help reduce inflammation in the brain and may delay the onset of Alzheimer's disease.

Berries: Rich in flavonoids, the natural pigments found in berries like strawberries, blueberries, blackberries, and mulberries, these fruits help reduce oxidative stress. An April 2012 study in the Annals of Neurology showed that women who consumed two or more servings of strawberries or blueberries each week delayed memory decline by up to two and a half years. Berries are also believed to boost learning and improve communication between brain cells.

Fatty Fish: These are high in Omega-3 fatty acids, including alpha-linolenic acid (ALA), eicosapentaenoic acid (EPA), and docosahexaenoic acid (DHA). Omega-3s are critical for building brain and nerve cells. Fatty fish include salmon, trout, herring, mackerel, albacore tuna, and sardines. However, be mindful of mercury and other toxins, especially in freshwater fish. Knowing what body of water it came from and what its tributaries are, can be valuable information in this respect.

Nuts and Seeds: These are high in protein, Omega-3 fatty acids, and antioxidants.[12] Walnuts, in particular, have been shown to improve cognitive function.[13] A 2015 UCLA study suggested improved cognitive test scores among people who consumed walnuts. Nuts and seeds also help lower blood pressure and clear your arteries, benefiting both your brain and heart.

Tea and Coffee: Both are high in antioxidants and offer the benefits of caffeine. Studies have shown that people who consume caffeine perform better on cognitive tests than those who do not.[14] A 2014 study in Journal of Nutrition found that higher levels of caffeine consumption were linked to improved mental function. However, caffeine has downsides, such as increased blood pressure, anxiety, insomnia, and the risk of osteoporosis, so moderation is key.

---

[12] Chauhan A, Chauhan V. Beneficial Effects of Walnuts on Cognition and Brain Health. Nutrients. 2020 Feb 20;12(2):550. doi: 10.3390/nu12020550. PMID: 32093220; PMCID: PMC7071526.

[13] Kevin M.R. Nijssen, Ronald P Mensink, Jagchum Plat, Peter J. Joris. Long-term mixed nut consumption improves brain vascular function and memory: A randomized, controlled crossover trial in older adults. Randomized Control Trials Volume 42 Issue, P1067-1075, July 2023

[14] Institute of Medicine (US) Committee on Military Nutrition Research; Marriott BM, editor. Food Components to Enhance Performance: An Evaluation of Potential Performance-Enhancing Food Components for Operational Rations. Washington (DC): National Academies Press (US); 1994. 20, Effects of Caffeine on Cognitive Performance, Mood, and Alertness in Sleep-Deprived Humans.

Oranges: Rich in Vitamin C, a potent antioxidant found in high concentrations within the brain. A 2017 study showed that vitamin C plays a role in neuronal differentiation, maturation, myelin formation, and modulating the cholinergic, catecholaminergic, and glutaminergic systems."[15] The study showed a strong relationship between vitamin C and cognitive development. Oranges are not commonly thought of in connection with brain wellness because they are non-fatty foods, but their main vitamin is essential for this most important organ.

Dark Chocolate: High in flavonoids, dark chocolate benefits the brain by accumulating in regions responsible for learning and memory, especially the hippocampus.[16] Dark chocolate also contains antioxidants and natural stimulants that help prevent memory decline. A study on older adults demonstrated better cognitive test performance among those

---

[15] Travica N, Ried K, Sali A, Scholey A, Hudson I, Pipingas A. Vitamin C Status and Cognitive Function: A Systematic Review. Nutrients. 2017 Aug 30;9(9):960. doi: 10.3390/nu9090960. PMID: 28867798; PMCID: PMC5622720.

[16] Sokolov AN, Pavlova MA, Klosterhalfen S, Enck P. Chocolate and the brain: neurobiological impact of cocoa flavanols on cognition and behavior. Neurosci Biobehav Rev. 2013 Dec;37(10 Pt 2):2445-53. doi: 10.1016/j.neubiorev.2013.06.013. Epub 2013 Jun 26. PMID: 23810791.

who consumed flavonoid-rich foods like wine, tea, and chocolate.[17]

Eggs: Rich in fats and nutrients essential for brain function and memory, eggs contain protein, iron, zinc, selenium, iodine, folate, vitamin A, choline, and long-chain polyunsaturated fatty acids 1 and 3. The yolk is particularly high in choline, which helps improve brain function and memory.

Whole grains have a low glycemic index, break down slowly, and release carbohydrates gradually into your bloodstream. Whole-grain breads are different from breads containing refined sugars, which are linked to lower levels of brain activity. Whole grains include brown rice, quinoa, oatmeal, whole-grain pasta, bread, and buckwheat.

Avocados are another food high in healthy fats. They have been shown to reduce blood pressure, which helps prevent cognitive decline. Avocados contain both healthy unsaturated fats and monounsaturated fats. As previously discussed, monounsaturated fats promote healthy blood flow, boosting brain health. Avocados also contain vitamin

---

[17] Nurk E, Refsum H, Drevon CA, Tell GS, Nygaard HA, Engedal K, Smith AD. Intake of flavonoid-rich wine, tea, and chocolate by elderly men and women is associated with better cognitive test performance. J Nutr. 2009 Jan;139(1):120-7. doi: 10.3945/jn.108.095182. Epub 2008 Dec 3. PMID: 19056649.

E, which may aid in preventing Alzheimer's disease, and folate, which can help fight depression.

Have you noticed a pattern in these foods, except for oranges? Most of these foods are categorized as fats. They tend to be high in healthy fats, which are beneficial for brain health.

The following are a few supplements that help keep the mind sharp. As with all supplements, consult your physician if you suffer from any chronic illness or take any medication. Many formulations on the market contain a mix of different chemicals. I will address some substances that may or may not be in those various marketed solutions. If you are interested in anything that contains a mixture of ingredients, always check the purity and the type of fillers used.

Resveratrol is an antioxidant found in berries. It helps protect cells from damage, slows cognitive decline, and improves blood flow to the brain. A 2017 study found that in the treatment of patients with Alzheimer's disease and stroke, "Resveratrol was beneficial in all three clinical trials presented, suggesting that resveratrol would be an effective treatment for neurological disorders."[18] Typical daily doses

[18] Berman AY, Motechin RA, Wiesenfeld MY, Holz MK. The therapeutic potential of resveratrol: a review of clinical trials. NPJ Precis

range from 50–500 milligrams (mg), though higher doses have been used in some studies.

L-theanine is an amino acid found in mushrooms and black teas. It is also available as a supplement to improve mental performance and focus. Studies on L-theanine have shown promising results in preventing cognitive decline.[19] A daily dose of 100 to 250 milligrams is recommended.

Ashwagandha is a natural shrub native to the Middle East and parts of Africa. A 2021 study demonstrated that individuals who took Ashwagandha capsules performed better in three cognitive skill domains: visual memory, new learning, and sustained attention.[20] Other studies have further shown Ashwagandha's ability to improve memory

---

Oncol. 2017;1:35. doi: 10.1038/s41698-017-0038-6. Epub 2017 Sep 25. PMID: 28989978; PMCID: PMC5630227.

[19] Foxe JJ, Morie KP, Laud PJ, Rowson MJ, de Bruin EA, Kelly SP. Assessing the effects of caffeine and theanine on the maintenance of vigilance during a sustained attention task. Neuropharmacology. 2012 Jun;62(7):2320-7. doi: 10.1016/j.neuropharm.2012.01.020. Epub 2012 Feb 2. PMID: 22326943.

[20] Gopukumar K, Thanawala S, Somepalli V, Rao TSS, Thamatam VB, Chauhan S. Efficacy and Safety of Ashwagandha Root Extract on Cognitive Functions in Healthy, Stressed Adults: A Randomized, Double-Blind, Placebo-Controlled Study. Evid Based Complement Alternat Med. 2021 Nov 30;2021:8254344. doi: 10.1155/2021/8254344. PMID: 34858513; PMCID: PMC8632422.

and cognitive skills. The daily dosage of Ashwagandha can be up to 1,000 mg per day.[21]

Phosphatidylserine, is a fat found naturally in brain tissue. This lipid is vital for communication throughout your nervous system, as it activates and releases neurotransmitters. Supplementation may help protect the brain and lower the risk of chronic brain diseases.[22] The typical daily dosage is 400 mg.

Omega-3 fatty acids have been mentioned several times already. Not only are they beneficial as a food source, but they are also a very healthy and helpful supplement. Omega-3 fatty acids reduce inflammation, especially in the brain, and may reduce the risk of cognitive decline, Alzheimer's disease, and dementia. These fatty acids are essential in the natural makeup of nerve cell membranes and help protect against neurodegeneration. Omega-3 fatty acid supplements are available in two forms: fish oils and processed oils. The fish oil variety is recommended as it is

---

[21] Choudhary D, Bhattacharyya S, Bose S. Efficacy and Safety of Ashwagandha (Withania somnifera (L.) Dunal) Root Extract in Improving Memory and Cognitive Functions. J Diet Suppl. 2017 Nov 2;14(6):599-612. doi: 10.1080/19390211.2017.1284970. Epub 2017 Feb 21. PMID: 28471731.

[22] Kim HY, Huang BX, Spector AA. Phosphatidylserine in the brain: metabolism and function. Prog Lipid Res. 2014 Oct;56:1-18. doi: 10.1016/j.plipres.2014.06.002. Epub 2014 Jun 30. PMID: 24992464; PMCID: PMC4258547.

more effective in its natural form. The usual dosage is 1,000 mg (1 gram) daily.

Creatine is well-known for athletic and muscular development, but it may also help with brain function. Creatine is an amino acid found in the brain and muscle tissues. A 2022 study stated, "There is a potential for creatine supplementation to improve cognitive processing."[23] Another study showed that supplementing with creatine could increase positive brain changes by up to 9.8%.[24] The International Society of Sports Nutrition recommends a daily dosage of 0.3 grams of creatine per kilogram of body weight.

Magnesium is involved in over 600 enzymatic processes in the body and is an important mineral for brain health. Cognitive ability has been shown to increase with

---

[23] Roschel H, Gualano B, Ostojic SM, Rawson ES. Creatine Supplementation and Brain Health. Nutrients. 2021 Feb 10;13(2):586. doi: 10.3390/nu13020586. PMID: 33578876; PMCID: PMC7916590.

[24] Lyoo IK, Kong SW, Sung SM, Hirashima F, Parow A, Hennen J, Cohen BM, Renshaw PF. Multinuclear magnetic resonance spectroscopy of high-energy phosphate metabolites in human brain following oral supplementation of creatine-monohydrate. Psychiatry Res. 2003 Jun 30;123(2):87-100. doi: 10.1016/s0925-4927(03)00046-5. PMID: 12850248.

higher magnesium intake, especially in women.[25] The RDA for magnesium is between 310 and 420 milligrams.

Ginkgo biloba is one of the oldest tree species, and its leaves are cultivated to make an extract. Ginkgo contains flavonoids, which are believed to benefit brain health. Ginkgo has long been considered a supplement for preventing memory decline and has shown quantifiable positive effects.[26, 27]A 2014 study from McGill University suggested that the best impact comes from taking 240 mg of Ginkgo biloba daily.

Selenium is a naturally occurring trace mineral that has shown promise in combating conditions such as Alzheimer's disease and multiple sclerosis. Selenium has antioxidant properties that protect the brain and reduce inflammation. A 2015 study found that "the role of selenium and

---

[25] Alateeq, K., Walsh, E.I. & Cherbuin, N. Dietary magnesium intake is related to larger brain volumes and lower white matter lesions with notable sex differences. Eur J Nutr 62, 2039–2051 (2023).

[26] Weinmann S, Roll S, Schwarzbach C, Vauth C, Willich SN. Effects of Ginkgo biloba in dementia: systematic review and meta-analysis. BMC Geriatr. 2010 Mar 17;10:14. doi: 10.1186/1471-2318-10-14. PMID: 20236541; PMCID: PMC2846949.

[27] Silberstein RB, Pipingas A, Song J, Camfield DA, Nathan PJ, Stough C. Examining brain-cognition effects of ginkgo biloba extract: brain activation in the left temporal and left prefrontal cortex in an object working memory task. Evid Based Complement Alternat Med. 2011;2011:164139. doi: 10.1155/2011/164139. Epub 2011 Aug 18. PMID: 21941584; PMCID: PMC3166615.

selenoproteins in neurotransmission might not only be limited to their antioxidant properties but also to inflammation."[28]

Over the past two chapters, we have focused on brain health and wellness. It is important to allow your brain, like the rest of your body, to reach its full genetic potential. In a later chapter, we will discuss the limitations of genetics, but that should not stop you from striving to be as fit as possible—whether over 50 or at any age.

Your brain is precious, and without it, all health declines. These past two chapters have provided solid information to help improve your cognitive ability and memory. The key point is to eat what is good for you and avoid what is not. Your body is a machine, and the brain is the coordination system. Keep it well-oiled, especially after the age of 50. Staying on track includes eating for a healthy body and a sharp mind.

---

[28] Solovyev ND. Importance of selenium and selenoprotein for brain function: From antioxidant protection to neuronal signaling. J Inorg Biochem. 2015 Dec;153:1-12. doi: 10.1016/j.jinorgbio.2015.09.003. Epub 2015 Sep 15. PMID: 26398431.

Chapter Eight: After Menopause

Women over the age of 50 understand menopause and the post-menopause stage. The end of a female's reproductive lifecycle typically occurs around 50, give or take a few years. During this time, there is a sharp decrease in the production of estrogen and progesterone, two essential hormones necessary for reproduction and aid in keeping a woman metabolically youthful. The body typically undergoes many physiological changes with the drop in estrogen and progesterone. During the process of menopausal changes, which can last from 2-8 years but usually lasts 4 years, these hormonal declines may cause unwanted symptoms such as hot flashes, night sweats, pain in the joints, changes in mood, and vaginal dryness.

Post menopause, when the menopause changes have completed, there are typically some adverse physiological effects that start to occur in a woman's body. Medicine defines the completion of menopause as one year after a female's last period, although hormonal testing, which is not usually required, can give the most definitive phase of completion. The most dramatic metabolic changes include loss of bone density and an increase in central abdominal fat. Other physiological changes include adverse cholesterol profiles and a decrease in vascular tone.[1] As estrogen decreases, the ratio of male androgens to female estrogen in female biochemistry shifts, possibly contributing to many changes, particularly in the cardiovascular system.[2]

Estrogen keeps your hair and skin well-hydrated and is important for collagen production.[3] Collagen is the protein responsible for keeping skin wrinkle-free and hair follicles nice and firm. These collagen changes will also affect hair and skin dryness. Another side effect of estrogen loss is the potential for facial hair. Research has stated that 38-55% of women can experience some level of incontinence after

---

[1] Davis SR, Lambrinoudaki I, Lumsden M, Mishra GD, Pal L, Rees M, et al. (April 2015). "Menopause." Nature Reviews. Disease Primers. 1 (1): 15004. doi:10.1038/nrdp.2015.4. PMID 27188659.

[2] Raj A, Chakole S, Agrawal S, Gupta A, Khekade H, Prasad R, Lohakare T, Wanjari M. The Impact of Menopause on Cardiovascular Aging: A Comprehensive Review of Androgen Influences. Cureus. 2023 Aug 16;15(8):e43569. doi: 10.7759/cureus.43569. PMID: 37719547; PMCID: PMC10503403.

[3] Brincat M, Kabalan S, Studd JW, Moniz CF, de Trafford J, Montgomery J. A study of the decrease of skin collagen content, skin thickness, and bone mass in the postmenopausal woman. Obstet Gynecol. 1987 Dec;70(6):840-5. PMID: 3120067.

menopause. [4,5] There are complex biochemical processes that create this biological alteration. Still, the bottom line is that the hormonal changes after menopause will create many "aging effects," both on internal physiology and outward appearance. If you compound these pathways with a harmful diet, exposure to environmental factors, or chronic health conditions, aging factors can multiply. Likewise, exercising, eating healthy, and practicing clean living can limit menopausal side effects.

The same actions take place should someone undergo a radical hysterectomy (removal of the uterus, cervix, and ovaries) before initiating menopause. A surgical or induced menopause, as it is more correctly called, will immediately put the person into menopause. Without the ovaries, estrogen or progesterone are not produced.

---

[4] Kołodyńska G, Zalewski M, Rożek-Piechura K. Urinary incontinence in postmenopausal women - causes, symptoms, treatment. Prz Menopauzalny. 2019 Apr;18(1):46-50. doi: 10.5114/pm.2019.84157. Epub 2019 Apr 9. PMID: 31114458; PMCID: PMC6528037.

[5] Russo E, Caretto M, Giannini A, Bitzer J, Cano A, Ceausu I, Chedraui P, Durmusoglu F, Erkkola R, Goulis DG, Kiesel L, Lambrinoudaki I, Hirschberg AL, Lopes P, Pines A, Rees M, van Trotsenburg M, Simoncini T. Management of urinary incontinence in postmenopausal women: An EMAS clinical guide. Maturitas. 2021 Jan;143:223-230. doi: 10.1016/j.maturitas.2020.09.005. Epub 2020 Sep 30. PMID: 33008675.

Now that we have discussed the unsettling aspects of menopause, we can create a starting point from where to begin while understanding every woman is not going to have the same symptoms or number of symptoms outlined above. The first thing to do is embrace age, which brings wisdom and experience. Menopause is a natural part of life, and the unwanted effects are just another life challenge. Men also deal with what some call "male menopause." Although the term is technically incorrect, a significant decrease in testosterone levels in men affects their bodies similarly. Combating these unwanted physical traits is why you are reading this book. We will discuss good strategies for your quest to be Fit Over 50!

Exercise

There are many reasons exercise is good for your body; an earlier chapter is dedicated to exercise. Regular workouts during menopause are a great way to not only keep your body moving while benefiting from everything we talked about in a previous chapter but also combat many of the issues that arise from menopause.[6]

---

[6] Isenmann E, Kaluza D, Havers T, Elbeshausen A, Geisler S, Hofmann K, Flenker U, Diel P, Gavanda S. Resistance training alters body composition in middle-aged women depending on menopause - A 20-week control trial. BMC Womens Health. 2023 Oct 6;23(1):526. doi:

Do not shy away from strength training. Lifting weights and using resistance bands or kettlebells are great post-menopausal exercises. One of the ill effects of menopause is a decrease in muscle strength and tone. Nothing will help you with muscle strength and tone better than strength training. You will be putting your muscles under constant stress and strain, where your body will naturally act to heal and repair.[7] In the previously mentioned chapter, we discussed tear and repair, all on the micro level. Weight training forces your muscles into this process to maintain your current tone or build muscle to improve or maintain shape. You are not too old to develop muscles; try it for a few weeks, and you will see exactly what I am talking about.

Strength training also keeps your metabolism running at a high speed. Hormonal drops may make you feel lethargic. One of the significant benefits of a higher metabolism is caloric expenditure, which results in maintaining or losing weight. You can and will lose weight by lifting weights. Even after you leave the gym and go about your day, your body will repair from the effects of your workout.

10.1186/s12905-023-02671-y. PMID: 37803287; PMCID: PMC10559623.

[7] Benedetti MG, Furlini G, Zati A, Letizia Mauro G. The Effectiveness of Physical Exercise on Bone Density in Osteoporotic Patients. Biomed Res Int. 2018 Dec 23;2018:4840531. doi: 10.1155/2018/4840531. PMID: 30671455; PMCID: PMC6323511.

Metabolism continues to work while expending calories. Regularly lifting heavy weights can stimulate various bodily systems, supporting healthy circulation and metabolism.

Strength training is one of the best ways to maintain bone loss, another effect of post-menopause. As mentioned earlier, a scientific principle known as Wolff's Law states that bones will adapt to the loads they are required to bear. Osteopenia and, ultimately, osteoporosis can be helped with load-bearing exercises such as strength training.[8] If you suffer from osteoporosis already, it is best to talk with your treating physician so you can safely begin a program and use the correct weight. Injury avoidance is critical; you can build bone density with proper guidance and good exercise mechanics.

Getting some type of cardiovascular exercise and strength training is also essential. Whether you play tennis, pickleball, or some other action sport, run, ride a bike, or dance, exercising your heart and lungs is critical.

Other aerobic or anaerobic exercise forms include HIIT (High-Intensity Interval Training), which provides short

---

[8] Varahra A, Rodrigues IB, MacDermid JC, Bryant D, Birmingham T. Exercise to improve functional outcomes in persons with osteoporosis: a systematic review and meta-analysis. Osteoporos Int. 2018 Feb;29(2):265-286. doi: 10.1007/s00198-017-4339-y. Epub 2018 Jan 6. PMID: 29306984

bursts, short rest, and performing multiple reps. For example, you may do battle ropes for 30 seconds and then 30 seconds rest 5 times. Or swim a fast lap across a pool, rest for a specific time, then swim across the pool again with the identical time rest, repeating for a certain number of intervals. HIIT exercises are anaerobic, pushing yourself for short bursts with a brief rest. They will work your heart, lungs, muscles and joints. There are many options, some more strenuous or complex than others. HIIT gives you a great workout in a short period.

As always, stretch before your exercise and cool down afterward. Pulled muscles, strained tendons, and sore joints are never good. Exercise in front of a mirror to make sure your mechanics are correct.

Dietary Combat

After menopause, nutrition becomes even more critical compared to your younger days. The goal is to fight, stay off, or delay the effects of aging. The hormonal changes and lack of estrogen can have an impact that adds up year after year. This includes increased oxidative stress, an imbalance between antioxidants and free radicals. Eating the right foods and taking good supplements is essential to bring that balance back to something healthy. It is assumed you have begun, will, or have already been exercising. Good nutrition not only adds to the benefits of exercising but will also help your body stay rejuvenated. Here are good food options that you can include in your diet. Fruits, vegetables, grains, and nuts should always be a significant part of any diet, including those postmenopausal. Try adding some of these options; you may find them helpful.

Chicken is a staple of many diets. It is a meal that contains many important vitamins, such as niacin, selenium, and vitamin B6. Although chicken is an everyday meal, it should be consumed in leaner portions. Chicken can be an important post-menopausal food.

Eggs are another great source of protein. They contain protein, iron, zinc, selenium, iodine, folate, vitamins A and D, choline, and long-chain polyunsaturated fatty acids, essential for improved energy and bone density. It's always good to leave some boiled eggs in the refrigerator to eat after a workout, as they provide the protein and vitamins needed to benefit fitness.

Salmon is high in omega-3 fatty acids and lower in mercury than most other fish. Salmon is also high in vitamins B2, B3, B5, B7, E, and selenium. It is recommended that you check on the source of the salmon and whether it is wild-caught or farm-raised. Farm-raised tends to have antibiotics, whereas wild does not.

Cheese is an excellent source of calcium and vitamin D. It also contains protein and Vitamin B12. However, limit certain cheeses, such as blue cheese, feta cheese, and parmesan cheese, which are high in sodium.

Mackerel is another heart-healthy oily fish high in omega-3 fatty acids, specifically EPA and DHA, which may help alleviate some symptoms of depression and anxiety. It is also high in protein and vitamin D, which support heart health and reduce inflammation. However, it is best to avoid King Mackerel, as it is high in mercury, whereas Atlantic and Jack are generally lower in mercury levels.

Soy is often implicated in raising estrogen levels in those eating it, but there has been no credible research that claims this. Soy contains isoflavones, which are a plant type of estrogen. It is chemically different from estrogen in humans and does not convert after consumption. Soy also does not have any adverse side effects that can come from having too much estrogen.[9] The truth about soy is that it is

---

[9] Gabrielle Viscardi, Songhee Back, Amna Ahmed, Shuting Yang, Sonia Blanco Mejia, Andreea Zurbau, Tauseef A Khan, Amanda Selk, Mark Messina, Cyril WC Kendall, David JA Jenkins, John L Sievenpiper, Laura Chiavaroli,

an excellent food because it does contain these isoflavones. These phytoestrogens (plant-estrogen) can help balance hormone levels and help alleviate hot flashes and mood swings. Soy contains vitamin D and calcium to support bone health.

Yogurt is another food rich in calcium and vitamin D and contains important probiotics. It also includes high-quality protein to help with muscle maintenance and support metabolic function.

Brussels sprouts are rich in Vitamin K and Vitamin C. It boosts your immune system and gives your hair and health some of that needed collagen. Like all vegetables, Brussels sprouts are a good source of fiber.

Strawberries are rich in antioxidants, which help ease and lessen oxidative stress. Berries such as strawberries and blueberries are rich in anthocyanins, which have shown promising studies to reduce the occurrence of heart attacks. Strawberries are also rich in Vitamin C, boosting your immune system and collagen production.

Effect of Soy Isoflavones on Measures of Estrogenicity: A Systematic Review and Meta-Analysis of Randomized Controlled Trials, Advances in Nutrition, 2024, 100327

Avocados are high in monounsaturated fats, the healthiest type of fats. They have been shown to help reduce inflammation and support heart health. Avocados are also high in Vitamins E, which is excellent for the skin, and K.

Almonds are also high in monounsaturated fats and omega-3 fatty acids. Like all nuts, they are high in fiber, which is excellent for digestive health. Almonds also contain Vitamin E, magnesium, and calcium. Although most nuts, especially when eaten raw, are incredibly healthy, almonds may be the best for postmenopause nutrition.

Green tea is high in catechin antioxidants, especially EGCG. It has been shown to help prevent some cancers[10], burn fat[11], and support brain health[12]. Green tea can also help

---

[10] Filippini T, Malavolti M, Borrelli F, Izzo AA, Fairweather-Tait SJ, Horneber M, Vinceti M. Green tea (Camellia sinensis) for the prevention of cancer. Cochrane Database Syst Rev. 2020 Mar 2;3(3):CD005004. doi: 10.1002/14651858.CD005004.pub3. PMID: 32118296; PMCID: PMC7059963.

[11] Rostamian Mashhadi, M., Hosseini, S.R.A. The interaction effect of green tea consumption and exercise training on fat oxidation, body composition and blood lipids in humans: a review of the literature. Sport Sci Health 19, 461–477 (2023).

[12] Ma YH, Wu JH, Xu W, Shen XN, Wang HF, Hou XH, Cao XP, Bi YL, Dong Q, Feng L, Tan L, Yu JT. Associations of Green Tea Consumption and Cerebrospinal Fluid Biomarkers of Alzheimer's Disease Pathology in Cognitively Intact Older Adults: The CABLE Study. J Alzheimers Dis. 2020;77(1):411-421. doi: 10.3233/JAD-200410. PMID: 32804140

reduce inflammation while protecting against oxidative stress.

As stated above, you cannot go wrong with most fruits, vegetables, grains, and nuts. It is essential, though, to avoid certain foods and ingredients. It goes without saying that "bad sugars" such as refined sucrose, high fructose corn syrup, and those found in typical junk food can elevate your LDL and create mood and blood chemistry abnormalities. Harmful sugars can also increase your risk for heart disease, certain cancers, and diabetes. An alternative is to eat healthy sugars such as those found in fruits. Those sugars are good for you, and the fruit has nutritious benefits.

Importantly, refrain from consuming salt. With the depletion of estrogen, post-menopausal women have shown an increase in blood pressure compared when compared to pre-menopause. Limiting the amount of sodium is particularly important as salt sensitivity is a common post-menopause symptom.[13]Although soy is a beneficial food, soy sauce may be something to avoid as it tends to be high in sodium.

---

[13] Kim JM, Kim TH, Lee HH, Lee SH, Wang T. Postmenopausal hypertension and sodium sensitivity. J Menopausal Med. 2014 Apr;20(1):1-6. doi: 10.6118/jmm.2014.20.1.1. Epub 2014 Apr 28. PMID: 25371885; PMCID: PMC4217569.

Other foods to avoid include spicy foods that contain capsaicin, the active ingredient in chili peppers. Capsaicin can trigger heat receptors, which may cause vasodilation, leading to hot flashes.

Alcohol is another one you should try to limit, as it affects your immune system and overworks your liver. It can increase your risk for osteoporosis and heart disease. Alcohol also exacerbates sleep patterns, which are already a typical post-menopausal complaint. The ability to detox alcohol lessens with age, especially after menopause. [14]

With all this said, be judicious about the quantity and quality of what you consume, as I have been professing moderation in real-world situations. Deprivation is not a badge of honor. There are always situations, such as parties, nights out, etc., where you will consume in a way that may not be the most healthy. By living a life focused on wellness, your body will tell you what it needs the day after. Do not allow yourself to feel guilt or that health is unattainable by indulging occasionally.

---

[14] Milic J, Glisic M, Voortman T, Borba LP, Asllanaj E, Rojas LZ, Troup J, Kiefte-de Jong JC, van Beeck E, Muka T, Franco OH. Menopause, ageing, and alcohol use disorders in women. Maturitas. 2018 May;111:100-109. doi: 10.1016/j.maturitas.2018.03.006. Epub 2018 Mar 13. PMID: 29673827.

Beneficial Supplements

There is an entire chapter on supplements and their many benefits. Rather than being redundant, below are some extra supplements that can help combat the aging process and its symptoms, which will be the focus of this list.

Ashwagandha, which we have already discussed, is the cognitive benefits of ashwagandha. Ashwagandha also helps moderate stress levels, which directly affect the adrenal glands. Higher cortisol levels can wreak havoc on your metabolism, affecting mood, unwanted weight gain, and sleep disruption. Ashwagandha will moderate cortisol levels and balance hormones while significantly improving those symptoms associated with a drop in estrogen.

CoQ10 (Coenzyme Q10) is a powerful antioxidant that naturally declines with age. CoQ10 supplementation benefits cardiovascular health as well as mood swings and depression. This powerful supplement may be found in some skin care products looking to take advantage of its cellular replenishment effects. Many medications will deplete your natural CoQ10, while supplementing will help you remain healthy.

Vitamin E is beneficial for skin health, reducing the risk of blood clots by widening blood vessels and slowing the progress of Alzheimer's disease. Vitamin E is also a potent antioxidant that helps symptoms such as hot flashes and vaginal changes. Combating dry skin and sun damage is always a challenge, especially postmenopausal. Vitamin E has repeatedly been shown to be a fantastic supplement for facing that challenge.

Vitamin C is excellent for your immune system and restores tissue damage. It is also a robust skin antioxidant. Vitamin C is crucial in producing collagen, benefiting both hair and skin.

Omega-3 Fatty Acids, as discussed earlier, have an effective anti-inflammatory effect that benefits cardiovascular health and lowers triglycerides. They are also powerful antioxidants that help with cognitive function. Omega-3s have shown themselves to be beneficial in mitigating night sweats and depression.

Turmeric contains the potent ingredient curcumin. It has strong antioxidant properties and provides anti-inflammatory benefits, helping with joint pain. Turmeric has been shown to aid in weight loss, while it benefits many issues with the gut, including diarrhea, nausea, and constipation. Turmeric benefits from the unwanted symptoms of brain fog and depression.

Magnesium, a mineral, has shown great promise in reducing high cortisol symptoms during postmenopause. Foods like avocados, dark chocolate, legumes, and nuts are all high in magnesium. Magnesium promotes relaxation and supports sleep.

Modern agricultural processes strip our food of nutrients. Although eating healthy and avoiding harmful foods is essential, supplementing has many benefits for fulfilling the needs created by modern cultivating practices. Vitamins are never a substitute for a healthy wellness diet; they supplement your nutrition.

How Cortisol Plays a Role

Cortisol, the stress hormone, can magnify many of the symptoms that occur after menopause. The adrenal glands produce cortisol and release this hormone during stress. There is a complex process as part of the hypothalamus-pituitary-adrenal complex involved in the body's stress response, but ultimately, cortisol is secreted from the adrenal glands. Pathological conditions alter cortisol regulation, such as when there is an overproduction of cortisol, called Cushing Syndrome, or a cortisol deficiency called Addison's Disease. Our discussion concerns higher cortisol levels that do not fall within the parameters of these two clinical disease processes. Instead, stress-related higher or sustained cortisol levels may create unwanted symptoms.

Cortisol is an essential hormone in your body's natural flight or fight response. Your adrenal glands will release cortisol during times of stress, a primal and instinctual reaction meant to keep you on high alert. Cortisol is also necessary for many healthy metabolic processes, such as blood pressure maintenance, immune responses, and the regulation of blood sugar levels. It is an important hormone, but cortisol can be detrimental at high or sustained levels.

After menopause, the levels of both estrogen and progesterone drop significantly. Both hormones, along with cortisol and, to a minor extent, testosterone, are all important as they work synergistically in moderating moods and sustaining normal homeostasis. Progesterone is a hormone that creates a more calming effect that can counter estrogen and cortisol in the stress sequence. With the conclusion of menopause, the adrenals will primarily deliver cortisol; this creates a situation where there isn't as much of a countering hormone to balance cortisol's effect.[15,16] Stress relief can become more complex without this balance.

A basic example is when many females encounter a steep drop in progesterone production before menstruation. This temporary reduction in production can affect mood, sleeping patterns, and other symptoms, creating what is commonly known as "Premenstrual Syndrome." [17,18] PMS symptoms will wane once progesterone returns as part of the natural menstrual cycle.

Elevated and sustained cortisol levels can adversely affect sleep, increase unwanted weight gain, decrease muscle mass, and may lead to heart disease as well as other

---

[15] Krolick KN, Shi H. Estrogenic Action in Stress-Induced Neuroendocrine Regulation of Energy Homeostasis. Cells. 2022 Mar 3;11(5):879. doi: 10.3390/cells11050879. PMID: 35269500; PMCID: PMC8909319

[16] Gaffey AE, Wirth MM. Stress, rejection, and hormones: Cortisol and progesterone reactivity to laboratory speech and rejection tasks in women and men. F1000Res. 2014 Sep 2;3:208. doi: 10.12688/f1000research.5142.2. PMID: 25580228; PMCID: PMC4288428.

[17] Lombardi I, Luisi S, Quirici B, Monteleone P, Bernardi F, Liut M, Casarosa E, Palumbo M, Petraglia F, Genazzani AR. Adrenal response to adrenocorticotropic hormone stimulation in patients with premenstrual syndrome. Gynecol Endocrinol. 2004 Feb;18(2):79-87. doi: 10.1080/09513590310001652955. PMID: 15195499.

[18] Monteleone P, Luisi S, Tonetti A, Bernardi F, Genazzani AD, Luisi M, Petraglia F, Genazzani AR. Allopregnanolone concentrations and premenstrual syndrome. Eur J Endocrinol. 2000 Mar;142(3):269-73. doi: 10.1530/eje.0.1420269. PMID: 10700721.

potential chronic diseases. Physiologically, the body should not be under prolonged or constant stress.

The basics in this book will provide some of the best ways to counter the overproduction of cortisol and the unwanted rise in stress. Resistance training, such as lifting weights, can boost endorphins, which help lower stress levels. Endorphins are your body's natural chemical that relieves pain and stress. Other exercises like HIIT, aerobics, and sports can also release endorphins.

On the contrary, excess endurance exercises, which deplete carbohydrates, can prompt your body to produce more cortisol, which triggers the liver to initiate gluconeogenesis. Exercise is good, but excessive exercise may initiate the stress complex, which can have a reverse effect than intended on cortisol production[19]. Be mindful if running, jogging, biking, or swimming for extended periods. While regular exercise is essential for maintaining health, subjecting the body to excessive physical stress or strain can be detrimental rather than beneficial

---

[19] Hill EE, Zack E, Battaglini C, Viru M, Viru A, Hackney AC. Exercise and circulating cortisol levels: the intensity threshold effect. J Endocrinol Invest. 2008 Jul;31(7):587-91. doi: 10.1007/BF03345606. PMID: 18787373.

Other activities stimulating endorphin release include creating music or listening to music. Relaxation techniques such as yoga, meditation, or massage help to trigger endorphins further. It has also been suggested that a hot bath and sunshine may also release your body endorphins.

Nutrition is essential in calming the cortisol effect. Eat healthy fats, green leafy vegetables, and fruits high in vitamins C and B. Getting in front of the cortisol issue while understanding its effects is necessary. Knowing how it plays a role and developing good personal strategies to stay in front of it is a healthy, natural approach. It is expected to have feelings of stress, anxiety, or depression after menopause. Natural and normal hormonal changes can, unfortunately, cause mood swings stimulating cortisol release. Spend some time finding effective relaxation techniques that work for you while caring for your physical well-being. This is all part of the natural and healthy process.

Hormone Therapy

Estrogen replacement therapy was once a prevalent treatment, but with new studies and the documentation of potential side effects, this once common form of therapy has now been limited.[20] As with all medication and potential treatment, this is a discussion between you and your physician. This book gives vital information on striving for your highest potential fitness over 50 and naturally confronting processes such as post-menopause. Whether you are on estrogen, other hormone replacement, or any medication, embracing the foundations found in this chapter will not only help you work toward health and wellness but will help to alleviate those symptoms. It is essential to give yourself every possible opportunity to live a peaceful, healthy, long life after menopause.

---

[20] Cho, Leslie & Kaunitz, Andrew & Faubion, Stephanie & Hayes, Sharonne & Lau, Emily & Pristera, Nicole & Scott, Nandita & Shifren, Jan & Shufelt, Chrisandra & Stuenkel, Cynthia & Lindley, Kathryn. (2023). Rethinking Menopausal Hormone Therapy: For Whom, What, When, and How Long?. Circulation. 147. 597-610. 10.1161/CIRCULATIONAHA.122.061559.

Chapter Nine: The Testosterone Dilemma

Common scientific understanding suggests that after age 40, natural testosterone levels in men decrease by about 1% yearly. Lower levels of testosterone can cause many adverse health issues, such as damage to the cardiovascular system, increased levels of unhealthy fat, decreased muscle tone, and lowered bone density. Low testosterone can also lead to fatigue, cholesterol metabolism issues, diabetes, and sexual dysfunction. As men age, testosterone levels naturally decline, and this drop may accelerate the overall aging process.[1,2] New evidence from 2024 suggests that testosterone levels are decreasing at a faster rate than previous generations experienced.[3] Although the exact cause

[1] Samoszuk, Michael & Morgentaler, Abraham & de Groot, Mark & Solinge, Wouter & Li, Yu & Adair, Fiona & Hoefer, Imo & Haitjema, Saskia. (2020). Association of low testosterone with changes in non-cardiovascular biomarkers in adult men. International Journal of Impotence Research. 32. 1. 10.1038/s41443-019-0112-4.

[2] Yassin A, Haider A, Haider KS, Caliber M, Doros G, Saad F, Garvey WT. Testosterone Therapy in Men With Hypogonadism Prevents Progression From Prediabetes to Type 2 Diabetes: Eight-Year Data From a Registry Study. Diabetes Care. 2019 Jun;42(6):1104-1111. doi: 10.2337/dc18-2388. Epub 2019 Mar 12. PMID: 30862651.

[3] Travison TG, Araujo AB, O'Donnell AB, Kupelian V, McKinlay JB. A population-level decline in serum testosterone levels in American

has not been identified, this decline can negatively affect overall health. That's why developing a comprehensive fitness plan is essential for combating potential testosterone decrease.

We've identified the problems associated with lower testosterone levels in men. It's not enough to merely identify the problem; we must explore solutions to reverse or slow this concerning trend. This chapter will look at natural approaches to combat lower testosterone levels. While acknowledging that some men may be genetically predisposed to lower testosterone due to pathological or inherited causes, we will focus on what can be done to maximize your efforts. This includes what substances to avoid, lifestyle changes, and ideas you may not have considered. Our goal is to be fit over 50, 60, 70, and beyond.

As this book emphasizes, fitness is not a single-element activity. It is not just about exercise, diet, or supplements. Fitness is a holistic combination of elements synergizing with your body's systems. Together, the foods you eat, the supplements you take, and how you exercise will have a cumulative effect on your overall health and fitness.

---

men. J Clin Endocrinol Metab. 2007 Jan;92(1):196-202. doi: 10.1210/jc.2006-1375. Epub 2006 Oct 24. PMID: 17062768.

Know Your Levels

It's important to start by knowing your testosterone levels rather than guessing or assuming. A test can determine both:

1. Free testosterone, which is unbound circulating testosterone, and
2. Total testosterone, which includes both attached and unbound/free testosterone—hence the term "total testosterone."

Free testosterone is more usable by your body because it is unbound by other compounds. About 98% of your testosterone is bound, while only around 2% is free.

There are two simple options for testing: at-home tests or blood tests conducted in a lab. While home tests can be convenient and reliable, a blood test analyzed by a lab is typically more accurate.

1. The average total testosterone range for a man under 50 is between 300 ng/dL and 836 ng/dL (nanograms per deciliter).
2. For males over 50, the average range is between 193 ng/dL and 740 ng/dL.

3. By comparison, women under 50 typically have levels between 15 ng/dL and 70 ng/dL, while women over 50 range from 2 ng/dL to 41 ng/dL.

Testosterone levels will vary over the course of the day. Studies show that men in their 30s can have 30–35 times higher total testosterone levels in the mid to late afternoon.[4] If your levels are abnormal, further tests may be recommended to determine if any underlying issues are contributing to this.

Lab tests for total testosterone are often included in a comprehensive blood panel, which evaluates other important blood chemistries. This is the most thorough way to identify your testosterone levels and other contributing factors.

What Can We Do?

Let's say you've identified that your testosterone levels are low, and no pathological processes are causing this. What can you do? First, address the issue naturally, starting by assessing your weight. Being overweight can decrease testosterone levels. Simply losing weight can improve testosterone levels. One study found that for every one-point increase in Body Mass Index (excess weight gained) BMI),

---

[4] Plymate SR et al. 1989 Journal of Andrology 10 366–371.

total testosterone levels decreased by 2%.[5] Another study in 2008 found that men just over 30 had a higher likelihood of lower testosterone levels based on waist circumference. An increase of 4 inches in waist circumference was associated with a 75% higher predictability of lower testosterone.[6]

A diet high in sugar can reduce free testosterone levels due to the body's response when insulin is released rapidly. High insulin levels decrease testosterone by turning off the genes responsible for producing sex hormone-binding globulin.[7,8] Diets that include sugary drinks and processed desserts can also lead to weight gain and insulin resistance,

---

[5] Thomas G. Travison, Andre B. Araujo, Varant Kupelian, Amy B. O'Donnell, John B. McKinlay, The Relative Contributions of Aging, Health, and Lifestyle Factors to Serum Testosterone Decline in Men, The Journal of Clinical Endocrinology & Metabolism, Volume 92, Issue 2, 1 February 2007, Pages 549–555,

[6] Hall SA, Esche GR, Araujo AB, Travison TG, Clark RV, Williams RE, McKinlay JB. Correlates of low testosterone and symptomatic androgen deficiency in a population-based sample. J Clin Endocrinol Metab. 2008 Oct;93(10):3870-7. doi: 10.1210/jc.2008-0021. Epub 2008 Jul 29. PMID: 18664536; PMCID: PMC2579652.

[7] Chen L, Xie YM, Pei JH, Kuang J, Chen HM, Chen Z, Li ZW, Fu XY, Wang L, Lai SQ, Zhang ST, Chen ZJ, Lin JX. Sugar-sweetened beverage intake and serum testosterone levels in adult males 20-39 years old in the United States. Reprod Biol Endocrinol. 2018 Jun 23;16(1):61. doi: 10.1186/s12958-018-0378-2. PMID: 29935533; PMCID: PMC6015465.

[8] Caronia LM, Dwyer AA, Hayden D, Amati F, Pitteloud N, Hayes FJ. Abrupt decrease in serum testosterone levels after an oral glucose load in men: implications for screening for hypogonadism. Clin Endocrinol (Oxf). 2013 Feb;78(2):291-6. doi: 10.1111/j.1365-2265.2012.04486.x. PMID: 22804876.

a precursor to Type II diabetes. Insulin resistance lowers free testosterone levels by suppressing the hypothalamic-pituitary-testicular (HPT) axis, an essential part of the endocrine system that regulates male reproductive functions.[9] This creates a cycle where excess weight, poor diet, and hormonal imbalance can lead to further reductions in testosterone levels.

As you lose weight, you'll naturally eat healthier foods, which will benefit your overall health. Unhealthy foods that contribute to weight gain also negatively affect your body's systems. Eating better will improve your weight and help your internal systems function more efficiently. Conversely, poor eating habits will contribute to weight gain and burden your body with excess sugars, fats, and toxins.

Which Exercises?

As discussed, the first step in regulating your testosterone levels is controlling your weight. This alone will have a positive effect on testosterone levels. Eating right and working out will help create a caloric deficit.

---

[9] Fui MN, Dupuis P, Grossmann M. Lowered testosterone in male obesity: mechanisms, morbidity and management. Asian J Androl. 2014 Mar-Apr;16(2):223-31. doi: 10.4103/1008-682X.122365. PMID: 24407187; PMCID: PMC3955331.

The best exercise method to increase testosterone levels is resistance training, particularly exercises targeting large muscle groups. Squats, deadlifts, bench presses, and overhead presses all work your larger muscles. A 2016 study found that working large muscle groups has a more significant impact on testosterone regulation than losing weight through diet alone.[10] You can significantly improve your testosterone levels by losing weight through diet and exercising your large muscle groups.

Our bodies have five large muscle groups: the hamstrings, quadriceps, gluteus maximus, pectorals, and latissimus dorsi. You can perform various exercises to target these muscles. Most exercises for these muscles involve using heavier weights with explosive action. As mentioned in a previous chapter, always be sure to warm up beforehand and cool down after your workout. Don't lift more than you can safely manage, use good form, and always have a spotter.

---

[10] Kumagai H, Zempo-Miyaki A, Yoshikawa T, Tsujimoto T, Tanaka K, Maeda S. Increased physical activity has a greater effect than reduced energy intake on lifestyle modification-induced increases in testosterone. J Clin Biochem Nutr. 2016 Jan;58(1):84-9. doi: 10.3164/jcbn.15-48. Epub 2015 Nov 27. PMID: 26798202; PMCID: PMC4706091.

There are many opinions on how often to exercise large muscle groups, how much to lift during each session, and how many rest days to take between workouts. Take these recommendations into account, but ultimately, base your routine on your abilities, body type, and lifestyle. However, remember that exercising large muscle groups will boost your testosterone levels,[11] so don't skip leg day.

Another type of exercise that can help increase testosterone is HIIT (high-intensity interval training).[12] HIIT involves short bursts of intense exercise followed by short rest periods. Examples include jumping rope, sprints, battle ropes, and various floor exercises, often led by a personal trainer. HIIT exercises are anaerobic, unlike endurance aerobic exercises such as long-distance running, which tend to raise cortisol levels, acting as an antagonist to testosterone. It's always best to supplement endurance training with resistance training to balance your fitness program and maintain testosterone levels.

---

[11] Yeo JK, Cho SI, Park SG, Jo S, Ha JK, Lee JW, Cho SY, Park MG. Which Exercise Is Better for Increasing Serum Testosterone Levels in Patients with Erectile Dysfunction? World J Mens Health. 2018 May;36(2):147-152. doi: 10.5534/wjmh.17030. Epub 2018 Jan 26. PMID: 29623694; PMCID: PMC5924956.

[12] Di Blasio A, Izzicupo P, Tacconi L, et al. Acute and delayed effects of high intensity interval resistance training organization on cortisol and testosterone production. The Journal of Sports Medicine and Physical Fitness. 2016 Mar;56(3):192-199. PMID: 25373470.

How Cortisol Plays a Role

Cortisol is a hormone produced and secreted by the adrenal glands. It increases blood sugar levels when your body needs it, such as when carbohydrates are lacking, through a process called gluconeogenesis. Your liver creates sugar from non-sugar compounds like amino acids and fats. Cortisol helps regulate blood sugar when carbohydrates are depleted, suppresses the immune system when needed to reduce inflammation, and aids in metabolizing sugars, fats, and amino acids to produce muscle energy. It also helps with electrolyte balance, memory, and more.

Cortisol is released by the adrenal glands as needed. In normal amounts, this is beneficial. However, when your body is under chronic stress, cortisol can negatively affect your body, including lowering testosterone levels. People who are constantly stressed, anxious, or depressed often have higher cortisol levels. Elevated cortisol can lead to weight gain, high blood pressure, Type II diabetes, and lowered testosterone levels. Cortisol inhibits testosterone by reducing the activity of the HPG (hypothalamus, pituitary, gonadal) axis and blocking important endocrine receptors.[13]

---

[13] Sherman GD, Lerner JS, Josephs RA, Renshon J, Gross JJ. The interaction of testosterone and cortisol is associated with attained status

If you're stressed, not getting enough sleep, eating poorly, or over-exercising with extreme endurance workouts, your cortisol levels may be elevated, and your testosterone levels reduced.

Excessive endurance exercise depletes circulating carbohydrates, prompting your body to produce more cortisol so the liver can perform gluconeogenesis. Repeated extreme endurance exercises elevate cortisol levels, reducing testosterone. Cortisol is vital for many functions, but chronic elevation from stressors can disrupt your body's metabolic balance.

Food

Eating well and losing weight are crucial for maintaining normal testosterone levels. Certain foods can also help balance testosterone levels.[14] Instead of focusing on a specific diet, here are some foods that fit into various eating plans.

---

in male executives. J Pers Soc Psychol. 2016 Jun;110(6):921-9. doi: 10.1037/pspp0000063. Epub 2015 Aug 24. PMID: 26302434.

[14] Pecora G, Sciarra F, Gangitano E, Venneri MA. How Food Choices Impact on Male Fertility. Curr Nutr Rep. 2023 Dec;12(4):864-876. doi: 10.1007/s13668-023-00503-x. Epub 2023 Oct 20. PMID: 37861951; PMCID: PMC10766669

Onions and garlic are rich in flavonoids, making them powerful antioxidants. Studies have shown that both garlic[15] and onions[16] can increase fertility, likely due to their high antioxidant properties. These foods fight inflammation and promote virility.

Shellfish such as crab, oysters, and lobster are natural sources of zinc, an essential mineral for testosterone production. While zinc deficiency is rare, shellfish can provide a natural boost. Fatty fish like tuna, salmon, and mackerel are rich in vitamin D, another critical nutrient for testosterone production.[17]

Green leafy vegetables, which have been discussed throughout this book, contain many essential nutrients, including magnesium. While magnesium may not be directly involved in testosterone production, it plays a role in reducing oxidative stress by balancing free radicals and

---

[15] Musavi, Hadis & Tabnak, Malihe & Sheini, Farzaneh & Bezvan, Maryam & Amidi, Fardin & Abbasi, Mojtaba. (2018). Effect of garlic (Allium sativum) on male fertility: a systematic review. Journal of Herbmed Pharmacology. 7. 306-312. 10.15171/jhp.2018.46.

[16] Banihani SA. Testosterone in Males as Enhanced by Onion (Allium Cepa L.). Biomolecules. 2019 Feb 21;9(2):75. doi: 10.3390/biom9020075. PMID: 30795630; PMCID: PMC6406961.

[17] Wrzosek M, Woźniak J, Włodarek D. The causes of adverse changes of testosterone levels in men. Expert Rev Endocrinol Metab. 2020 Sep;15(5):355-362. doi: 10.1080/17446651.2020.1813020. Epub 2020 Oct 20. PMID: 33076711.

antioxidants.[18] A study demonstrated that testosterone levels increased in athletes supplemented with magnesium.[19]

Cocoa, especially dark chocolate, is also a good source of magnesium. It contains flavonoid antioxidants like quercetin and apigenin, which can improve fasting plasma glucose levels and insulin resistance.[20] This helps reduce the adrenal overproduction of cortisol.

Let's also not forget the importance of **healthy fats**. Avocados and egg yolks are two sources of such fats that support testosterone production. Avocados contain magnesium and boron, while egg yolks are high in protein, vitamin D, and selenium.

---

[18] Maggio M, Ceda GP, Lauretani F, Cattabiani C, Avantaggiato E, Morganti S, Ablondi F, Bandinelli S, Dominguez LJ, Barbagallo M, Paolisso G, Semba RD, Ferrucci L. Magnesium and anabolic hormones in older men. Int J Androl. 2011 Dec;34(6 Pt 2):e594-600. doi: 10.1111/j.1365-2605.2011.01193.x. Epub 2011 Jun 15. PMID: 21675994; PMCID: PMC4623306.

[19] Cinar V, Polat Y, Baltaci AK, Mogulkoc R. Effects of magnesium supplementation on testosterone levels of athletes and sedentary subjects at rest and after exhaustion. Biol Trace Elem Res. 2011 Apr;140(1):18-23. doi: 10.1007/s12011-010-8676-3. Epub 2010 Mar 30. PMID: 20352370.

[20] Leyva-Soto A, Chavez-Santoscoy RA, Lara-Jacobo LR, Chavez-Santoscoy AV, Gonzalez-Cobian LN. Daily Consumption of Chocolate Rich in Flavonoids Decreases Cellular Genotoxicity and Improves Biochemical Parameters of Lipid and Glucose Metabolism. Molecules. 2018 Sep 1;23(9):2220. doi: 10.3390/molecules23092220. PMID: 30200398; PMCID: PMC6225491.

The berry family is also important and rich in many nutrients that help with testosterone production. For example, blueberries and strawberries are high in quercetin and other flavonoids. Red meat is beneficial as well, as it is rich in zinc and aids in muscle mass production.

Lastly, **white button mushrooms** are excellent for testosterone production. These mushrooms are high in nutrients such as protein and antioxidants and are a non-animal source of vitamin D. If you follow a vegan or vegetarian diet, white button mushrooms should be included in your meals. They are low in calories and contain no fat. Importantly, they inhibit the production of aromatase, an enzyme that converts male hormones to female hormones.[21]

Some foods have been implicated in reducing testosterone levels. More research is needed to confirm their impact, but anecdotal evidence suggests they might play a role. I'll list a few foods that have been implicated, either rightly or wrongly. The most commonly discussed—and sometimes controversial—food is soy and soy-based products. This has become a common food choice for vegans and those looking to limit their intake of animal products.

---

[21] Patel S. Disruption of aromatase homeostasis as the cause of a multiplicity of ailments: A comprehensive review. J Steroid Biochem Mol Biol. 2017;168:19-25. doi:10.1016/j.jsbmb.2017.01.009

Soy can be used as a substitute for many foods, including dairy products, and is an ingredient in many "fake meats." Soy is high in protein and contains isoflavones, which are plant estrogens. Soy is rich in many nutrients, including B vitamins, potassium, and magnesium, and is high in complete proteins. Although soy has been accused of raising estrogen levels in males, research has not supported this claim.[22]

Mint tea has also been implicated in decreasing testosterone levels. While there have been some studies, most were either animal studies or studies not tested on males.[23,24] Flaxseeds, a common ingredient in energy bars and healthy snacks, are another food that has been implicated. Flaxseeds are high in polyphenols called lignans,

---

[22] Hamilton-Reeves JM, Vazquez G, Duval SJ, Phipps WR, Kurzer MS, Messina MJ. Clinical studies show no effects of soy protein or isoflavones on reproductive hormones in men: results of a meta-analysis. Fertil Steril. 2010 Aug;94(3):997-1007. doi: 10.1016/j.fertnstert.2009.04.038. Epub 2009 Jun 12. PMID: 19524224.

[23] Grant P. Spearmint herbal tea has significant anti-androgen effects in polycystic ovarian syndrome. A randomized controlled trial. Phytother Res. 2010 Feb;24(2):186-8. doi: 10.1002/ptr.2900. PMID: 19585478.

[24] Sadeghi Ataabadi M, Alaee S, Bagheri MJ, Bahmanpoor S. Role of Essential Oil of Mentha Spicata (Spearmint) in Addressing Reverse Hormonal and Folliculogenesis Disturbances in a Polycystic Ovarian Syndrome in a Rat Model. Adv Pharm Bull. 2017 Dec;7(4):651-654. doi: 10.15171/apb.2017.078. Epub 2017 Dec 31. PMID: 29399556; PMCID: PMC5788221.

which can bind to testosterone and accelerate its removal from the body.[25]

Trans fats are bad for you, no matter the topic, as we discussed in previous chapters. In addition to all the previously discussed issues, they have also been shown to reduce testosterone levels.[26] Long-term alcohol consumption has also been linked to decreased testosterone levels.[27,28] While small amounts of alcohol may increase testosterone levels, long-term and heavy use has a detrimental effect.

---

[25] Demark-Wahnefried W, Price DT, Polascik TJ, Robertson CN, Anderson EE, Paulson DF, Walther PJ, Gannon M, Vollmer RT. Pilot study of dietary fat restriction and flaxseed supplementation in men with prostate cancer before surgery: exploring the effects on hormonal levels, prostate-specific antigen, and histopathologic features. Urology. 2001 Jul;58(1):47-52. doi: 10.1016/s0090-4295(01)01014-7. PMID: 11445478.

[26] MInguez-Alarcón L, Chavarro JE, Mendiola J, Roca M, Tanrikut C, Vioque J, Jørgensen N, Torres-Cantero AM. Fatty acid intake in relation to reproductive hormones and testicular volume among young healthy men. Asian J Androl. 2017 Mar-Apr;19(2):184-190. doi: 10.4103/1008-682X.190323. PMID: 27834316; PMCID: PMC5312216.

[27] Vatsalya V, Liaquat HB, Ghosh K, Mokshagundam SP, McClain CJ. A review on the sex differences in organ and system pathology with alcohol drinking. Curr Drug Abuse Rev. 2016;9(2):87-92. doi:10.2174/1874473710666170125151410

[28] Erol A, Ho AM, Winham SJ, Karpyak VM. Sex hormones in alcohol consumption: a systematic review of evidence. Addict Biol. 2019 Mar;24(2):157-169. doi: 10.1111/adb.12589. Epub 2017 Dec 27. PMID: 29280252; PMCID: PMC6585852.

Licorice root is another product connected to lowering testosterone levels. The main ingredient in licorice, glycyrrhizin, affects androgen hormone levels, which are important for testosterone production. Licorice is commonly used in candies and sweeteners, and long-term use has shown statistical testosterone alterations.[29]

Supplements

Above, we discussed magnesium, quercetin, and other flavonoids. Now, let's look at herbs that may boost testosterone production. The first is Epimedium, also known as horny goat weed. It contains a compound called icariin, which is similar to chemicals used in the medical treatment of impotence.

The next herb is Ashwagandha. This herb is known for reducing stress and helping to lower cortisol levels. As discussed earlier, cortisol and testosterone are antagonistic, with their levels often being inversely related. Another herb is Malaysian ginseng, the root extract of which has been used to enhance testosterone levels. Puncturevine, which grows as a common weed, may stimulate luteinizing hormone, a

---

[29] Armanini D, Bonanni G, Mattarello MJ, Fiore C, Sartorato P, Palermo M. Licorice consumption and serum testosterone in healthy man. Exp Clin Endocrinol Diabetes. 2003 Sep;111(6):341-3. doi: 10.1055/s-2003-42724. PMID: 14520600.

precursor to testosterone. Another herb, Tongkat ail, also known as Ali's Walking Stick, is attributed to increased levels of testosterone. Yet another herb known as Fenugreek may inhibit the conversion of testosterone into estrogen. As with all supplements, especially herbs, if you are taking any medications, you should consult your physician before starting anything new.

A non-herb supplement that can help with testosterone is NAD (nicotinamide adenine dinucleotide), a natural compound found in our bodies that plays a vital role in testosterone synthesis. NAD is essential for the production of the enzyme 3β-Hydroxysteroid Dehydrogenase, which is required for synthesizing many hormones, including testosterone. As we age, our organic NAD levels decrease, and supplementing may help maintain healthy testosterone levels.

One important consideration is that if your testosterone levels are normal and you supplement to increase them unnecessarily, you could develop a "roid rage"-like syndrome. "Roid rage" is a term used for those on anabolic steroids who may experience fits of rage. Although this may not be as extreme as someone on illicit steroids, it has been reported that increasing testosterone unnecessarily can lead to irritability and aggression. This is why it's important to check your levels before starting any supplement regimen.

Many pre-packaged supplements come and go on the market. Some may work, some may not, and some may be better than others. The suggestion is always to read the label to see what's in these compounds. While I can't review every product, it's essential to do your homework. Are the ingredients a good mix? Do they combine fat-soluble substances with water-soluble chemicals? How long have they been on the market, and is there research with precise results? This book contains many citations because, when dealing with science, it's important to back up statements with reliable sources.

When All Else Fails?

This book focuses on natural health and staying healthy and fit over 50, 60, 70, and beyond. If you're doing everything naturally but still suffer from low testosterone, remember that everyone's body is different and responds differently to exercise and diet. If you're considering testosterone replacement therapy, consult a medical doctor. There are various types of treatments available, but that is a decision to be made between you and your doctor.

No matter how you choose to boost testosterone—whether through diet, supplements, or replacement therapy—always start by knowing your numbers. This is your decision, but if you supplement or go the medicinal route, make sure you continue eating right and exercising. You should never expect a pill to fix everything. A pill may help regulate your testosterone levels, but it won't make you fit. Fitness is cumulative; every part must be addressed and included in your journey, which is crucial for managing the testosterone dilemma effectively.

Chapter Ten: Those Important Incidentals

We've discussed nutrition, exercise, and other important aspects of being fit, but many "other things" can be included in your journey. Sometimes, adding or even tweaking your routine can make a significant difference. These are the incidentals you may not have thought about or were never introduced to, but they could bring about noticeable changes. Some may seem very simple, others take a little effort, while new ideas may present more of a challenge and fun endeavor. I've deliberately avoided addressing smoking, tobacco, vaping, etc., as it has been widely known for decades that smoking is unhealthy in every way. If you are a smoker, you're engaging in one of the worst practices for aging and damaging your chances for fitness.

As you read this chapter, keep taking notes and implementing some of these suggestions, which will positively impact your health and fitness.

Rest

Getting enough sleep or rest seems very difficult nowadays, yet sleep is a key component of staying fit and healthy.[1] Sleep is essential for recovery: it helps regulate hormones, restores your brain, resets your cells, and recharges your energy. Few things are as satisfying as a full night of restful sleep. The key phrase here is a full night of restful sleep.

A 2023 Gallup poll revealed that 43% of people felt they did not get enough sleep. Another poll conducted by OnePoll suggested that only 36% of those surveyed were satisfied with the amount of sleep they got. This means many people are walking around tired and not getting the rest they need for their health. The reasons cited in these polls included anxiety, constant thoughts, worries, and simply, "I can't sleep."

It is recommended that adults get 7–9 hours of sleep each night, and those over 65 should aim for 7–8 hours. Some researchers believe that napping during the day is not a good idea, as naps can interfere with nighttime sleep, while

---

[1] Vyazovskiy VV. Sleep, recovery, and metaregulation: explaining the benefits of sleep. Nat Sci Sleep. 2015 Dec 17;7:171-84. doi: 10.2147/NSS.S54036. PMID: 26719733; PMCID: PMC4689288.

others think that naps help recharge the mind and body. The National Sleep Foundation recommends a 20–30-minute nap to restore energy without putting you into a deep sleep. Napping for too long can affect your regular sleep rhythms by causing what is called *sleep inertia*. Once you fall asleep, your brain goes through sleep cycles, and a longer nap can disrupt your normal cycles.

To avoid entering deep sleep, set an alarm before you doze off and keep the nap to the 20–30-minute limit. Upon waking, eat a piece of fruit or drink some juice to give your body a quick boost of healthy sugar to energize yourself. Your brain needs rest, and there's nothing wrong with giving it a few minutes each day to recharge.

A 2017 research study[2] found inconclusive evidence on whether napping improves overall health, and other studies have produced similar results. However, on a purely anecdotal note, if you feel like you need a nap before a workout, bike ride, or any other healthy activity, it can help. Professional hockey players, for example, often nap before heading to the rink for a game. Without a nap, you might

---

[2] Mantua J, Spencer RMC. Exploring the nap paradox: are mid-day sleep bouts a friend or foe? Sleep Med. 2017 Sep;37:88-97. doi: 10.1016/j.sleep.2017.01.019. Epub 2017 Mar 6. PMID: 28899546; PMCID: PMC5598771.

skip the activity or not give it your best effort. Naps are fine, but as mentioned, be mindful of whether they affect your regular nighttime routine.

Rest is also important on a macro level. This includes time off from work, rest on weekends, and opportunities to unwind and reset. Our brains become congested with daily thoughts and stress, while our bodies grow fatigued from work and routines. Many articles have highlighted the importance of vacations or staycations for health, wellness, and fitness. It's easy to overlook the need to "stop and smell the roses" while caught up in your routine. Some people accumulate vacation time but never use it, thinking they're too indispensable at work or that taking time off makes them feel lazy. Taking time off doesn't have to mean an elaborate vacation; it could be time spent at home resting, enjoying family, hobbies, or simply doing nothing. All of this benefits your mind, body, and soul.

Rest is equally important for your exercise schedule. On exercise days, you exercise; on rest days, you rest. You can still stretch, take a light walk, or do some restorative yoga on those off days, but avoid pushing yourself to exercise "just a little." It's crucial to allow your body time to heal and recover.

Taking a week off from regular exercise every few months can be beneficial for recovery, especially for those who work out hard without skipping sessions. This is a common practice for athletes at the end of their season, where they take a week or even up to a month off, depending on the physical demands of their sport. Gains are made when the body rests between workouts, and recharging and recovery are essential—don't take them for granted.

Water

Our planet is roughly 71% water. The human body is, on average, 60% water but can vary from 45% to 75%. Around 20% of our food is water. Consequently, water is incredibly important. It is essential for regulating body temperature, enabling most cellular functions and nutrient absorption, and critical for eliminating waste. Water keeps your blood vessels open, allowing nutrients to be transported and waste to be carried to the kidneys. Without sufficient water, your kidneys cannot effectively remove toxins. Water also helps eliminate waste through perspiration and bowel movements. Lack of water or dehydration can lead to toxin buildup, impairing normal bodily functions.

A decrease in water consumption can lead to kidney stones. It's important to take in enough water to "bathe" the inside of your kidneys, helping them do their job. An environment with an excessive waste-to-water ratio harms both your kidneys and overall health. The kidneys act as a perfect filter for inorganic toxins, excess substances, and waste, but they need sufficient water to function properly.

Without enough water, you not only retain toxins in your body but may also suffer from various symptoms, such as lack of concentration, tiredness, irritability, headaches, dry skin, dark circles under the eyes, and weight retention. Extended dehydration can lead to fever, chills, a slow heart rate, weakness, dizziness, diarrhea, fatigue, and even death.

Water is important to drink not only when exercising or working in a hot environment but also throughout your regular day. The U.S. National Academies of Science, Engineering, and Medicine recommend that men consume 15.5 cups (3.7 liters) of fluid per day and women consume 11.5 cups (2.7 liters). To put this in perspective, a typical water bottle contains about two cups, which means men should aim for 7–8 bottles of water and women 5–6 bottles daily. That's a lot of water! So, what other options are there?

You can consume water through your food; all fruits and vegetables have abundant water content. Contrary to what many think, vegetables contain more water than fruits.

Including plant-based foods in your diet helps you meet your daily water needs while providing nutritional benefits. Most meats are also high in water content, ranging from 50% to 60% water.

When you exercise, your water intake needs to increase due to the higher demand you're placing on your body. Your metabolism speeds up, and you need to replace the fluids you burn and sweat out during workouts. This need for hydration includes training or playing in cold weather, where people may not feel thirsty in the traditional sense. It's easy to overlook hydration in cold environments, but cramping can occur from lack of water. Remember to stay hydrated regardless of the climate.

Some people claim that water consumption helps skin look younger, but there isn't conclusive scientific evidence to support this. Ana Gunn, a registered nurse and Clinic Director at Mia La Maven wellness and aesthetic clinic in Los Angeles, CA, says, "No matter how much water you drink, you can't hydrate away wrinkles." Board Certified Dermatologist Dr. Kimberly Jerdan adds, "The theory that drinking water prevents wrinkles or signs of aging is false."[3] However, some research suggests that staying hydrated may

---

[3] Bodi March 26, 2023 Beachbodyondemand.com

positively impact skin hydration and biomechanical behavior.[4] Anecdotal evidence also suggests that water helps prevent dark circles under the eyes and dry skin, which can contribute to a youthful appearance.

Balance

As we age, our natural postural balance tends to decline due to factors like changes in vision, decreases in muscle mass, and reduced joint flexibility. Balance issues can lead to falls, creating apprehension and limiting movement, which may further contribute to chronic diseases. It's essential to do everything possible to maintain or improve balance and proprioception.

There are a few ways to improve or at least maintain balance. The most important is to follow a regular exercise routine. Movement is life, and activities like walking, dancing, swimming, chair yoga, and tai chi can help improve strength, flexibility, and, ultimately, balance. Strong leg muscles are essential for maintaining balance, so it's vital to

---

[4] Palma L, Marques LT, Bujan J, Rodrigues LM. Dietary water affects human skin hydration and biomechanics. Clin Cosmet Investig Dermatol. 2015 Aug 3;8:413-21. doi: 10.2147/CCID.S86822. PMID: 26345226; PMCID: PMC4529263.

keep them strong with exercises like squats, lunges, and leg presses.

You can also incorporate balance exercises into your daily routine. Exercises such as standing on one foot, walking heel-to-toe, or using a foam pad or wobbleboard are excellent options. Try these exercises with your eyes open and then closed to challenge other parts of your brain.

Other exercises, like yoga or Pilates, focus on the core and help with flexibility, which also benefits balance. Improving core strength stabilizes the lower back and enhances posture. It's important to focus on keeping your body aligned, particularly over your feet. Leaning forward, which becomes more common with age, changes your center of gravity and affects movement, often starting from a poor position. Poor posture requires your brain to adapt, altering normal motion.

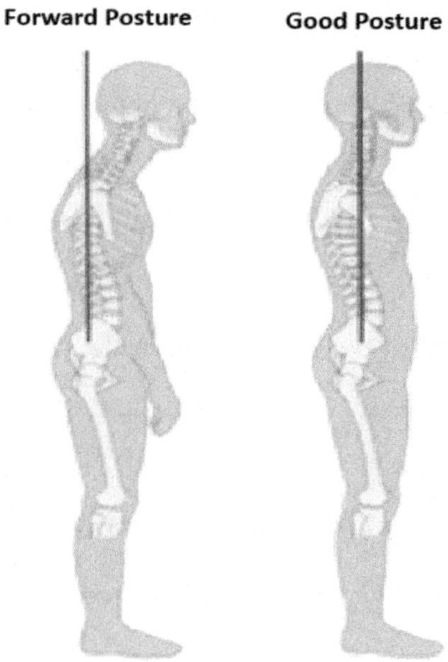

Wear the correct footwear. No matter how comfortable you think an old pair of worn shoes may be, shoes that are worn down on any part of their sole will affect your natural gait. When training, wear the right shoes for each activity, such as sneakers. Sneakers are also activity-specific, such as those for running, CrossFit, basketball, etc. Remember the importance of proper footwear and its impact on balance.

Balance is essential when it comes to staying fit. Besides the obvious consequence of falling, it's important not to be apprehensive about pursuing your desired activities while maintaining overall stability.

Alcohol

Recent studies[5,6] have shown that any amount of alcohol is harmful to your health. Ethyl alcohol is a known carcinogen[7,8] and can cause issues with your cardiovascular system, contribute to weight gain, and (as previously discussed) adversely affect testosterone levels with heavy use. Over 140,000 deaths each year are related to alcohol.[9] That's the cold reality, but it's not realistic to think everyone will stop drinking alcohol because of this information. This book deals with real-world situations and how to stay fit

---

[5] Biddinger KJ, Emdin CA, Haas ME, Wang M, Hindy G, Ellinor PT, Kathiresan S, Khera AV, Aragam KG. Association of Habitual Alcohol Intake With Risk of Cardiovascular Disease. JAMA Netw Open. 2022 Mar 1;5(3):e223849. doi: 10.1001/jamanetworkopen.2022.3849. Erratum in: JAMA Netw Open. 2022 Apr 1;5(4):e2212024. PMID: 35333364; PMCID: PMC8956974.

[6] IARC Working Group on the Evaluation of Carcinogenic Risks to Humans. Alcohol consumption and ethyl carbamate. IARC Monographs on the Evaluation of Carcinogenic Risks in Humans 2010; 96:3–1383.

[7] Goding Sauer A, Fedewa SA, Bandi P, Minihan AK, Stoklosa M, Drope J, Gapstur SM, Jemal A, Islami F. Proportion of cancer cases and deaths attributable to alcohol consumption by US state, 2013-2016. Cancer Epidemiol. 2021 Apr;71(Pt A):101893. doi: 10.1016/j.canep.2021.101893. Epub 2021 Jan 19. PMID: 33477084.

[8] IARC Working Group on the Evaluation of Carcinogenic Risks to Humans. Personal habits and indoor combustions. Volume 100 E. A review of human carcinogens. IARC Monographs on the Evaluation of Carcinogenic Risks in Humans 2012; 100(Pt E):373–472.

[9] Esser MB, Leung G, Sherk A, et al. Estimated Deaths Attributable to Excessive Alcohol Use Among US Adults Aged 20 to 64 Years, 2015 to 2019. JAMA Netw Open. 2022;5(11):e2239485. doi:10.1001/jamanetworkopen.2022.39485

naturally over 50. Most people enjoy a cocktail or beer, so when does alcohol begin to affect your fitness? Putting aside the first few statements in this section, which are true—that any amount of alcohol is bad for you—let's explore how much alcohol can be consumed while still maintaining fitness.

Let's first examine the harmful effects of alcohol before coming up with strategies to stay healthy. Most people know that alcohol can affect your liver, the body's largest detoxification organ. The liver is highly regenerative, meaning it can recover from most damage until scarring and long-term disease develop. The liver detoxifies alcohol by turning it into water and carbon dioxide through a process called oxidation. If the liver is overrun by alcohol, toxins can build up, limiting the organ's full effectiveness. When this happens regularly, the liver becomes hampered and unable to perform its other functions efficiently. Over time, this process adds to aging, as toxins are not properly expelled from the body.

One of the byproducts of alcohol metabolism is acetaldehyde. Although present in the body only briefly, it is a carcinogen. Alcohol is primarily broken down in the liver, but it can also be synthesized in the brain and pancreas. In the pancreas, the release of this toxic chemical can interfere with digestion. The pancreas produces enzymes and hormones essential for the breakdown and absorption of nutrition. Heavy drinking can also cause pancreatitis, an inflammation of the pancreas.[10]

Excessive alcohol consumption can weaken the heart, cause irregular heartbeats, raise blood pressure, and increase heart rate. Although some claim that red wine is good for the heart, it's not the alcohol itself that's beneficial—it's the grapes that contain resveratrol, an antioxidant we discussed in earlier chapters. Alcohol may also cause water retention, increasing pressure on the arteries and heart.

Drinking can weaken the immune system; even occasional binge drinking affects immunity. It takes a full 24 hours for your body to clear alcohol after a night of partying. The more you drink, the more your immune system suffers. Similarly, alcohol irritates the digestive system, affecting how it processes food, which is why people may experience diarrhea after a night of heavy drinking.

Now that we've covered the ugly side of alcohol, what can you do? Alcohol is a diuretic, which means it increases urine production, taking fluid out of your body. A hangover

---

[10] Rodriguez FD, Coveñas R. Biochemical Mechanisms Associating Alcohol Use Disorders with Cancers. Cancers. 2021; 13(14):3548. https://doi.org/10.3390/cancers13143548

is primarily caused by dehydration. The best way to combat a hangover is to rehydrate and restore electrolytes. Vitamin B6 can also help, as alcohol depletes this important vitamin while acting as a diuretic. Here's the catch-22: alcohol removes B6, but your body needs B6 to help detoxify. You need to replenish this vital vitamin after drinking.

So, how can you apply this information in your daily life? First, recognize that alcohol, in any amount, is not healthy for you, as outlined above. If you're a heavy drinker, take another look at the negative effects and understand that alcohol won't help you become fit over 50. If you're a light to moderate drinker, your body still needs to be in top shape to combat alcohol's effects. All levels of alcohol consumption dehydrate the body, affect organs, dry out skin, and can cause premature graying and under-eye circles. It's important to be mindful of your nutrition and supplementation. Hydrate regularly and consider a periodic water fast to help your body detox. Exercise, move your muscles and get your metabolism burning, but remember that you can't sweat alcohol out of your body. Only your liver can detoxify alcohol, so all you can do is be patient, hydrate, take B6, and wait it out.

This section may not be fun to read, but it's a dose of reality. While no judgment is passed, the information is crucial, and what you do with it is up to you. If your goal is to be fit over 50, it's your choice to create a strategy that aligns with that goal.

Stress

"Relax," they say. "Get your mind off of it," they add. The best advice always seems to come from someone who isn't in your shoes. Stress is natural; stress is life. Without stress, we'd be living in an imaginary world. How you deal with your stressors can help prevent stress from accelerating the aging process.

Stress has been scientifically proven to accelerate the aging process.[11,12] It also affects the brain, cardiovascular system, digestive system, vision, and hearing. Stress damages DNA by creating a constant state of inflammation.[13] We know stress isn't good for us, so what can we do to manage and combat it?

---

[11] Galluzzi, L., Yamazaki, T. & Kroemer, G. Linking cellular stress responses to systemic homeostasis. Nat Rev Mol Cell Biol 19, 731–745 (2018).

[12] Harvanek, Z.M., Fogelman, N., Xu, K. et al. Psychological and biological resilience modulates the effects of stress on epigenetic aging. Transl Psychiatry 11, 601 (2021).

[13] Yegorov YE, Poznyak AV, Nikiforov NG, Sobenin IA, Orekhov AN. The Link between Chronic Stress and Accelerated Aging. Biomedicines. 2020 Jul 7;8(7):198. doi: 10.3390/biomedicines8070198. PMID: 32645916; PMCID: PMC7400286.

A whole profession is dedicated to addressing stress, and medications are often prescribed. This section is not intended to trivialize the experience of those who suffer from clinical depression or anxiety. Instead, it is geared toward the general public, especially those over 50 who want to stay fit and manage their concerns—whether it's bills, kids, grandkids, or other important issues—by finding strategies to handle stress.

Managing stress takes many forms. Some people meditate to find peace by calming their minds. Meditation helps reprogram the brain, making it easier to manage life's stresses. A December 2023 article by the Mayo Clinic titled Meditation of Simple Fast Way to Reduce Stress stated, "Meditation can give you a sense of calm, peace, and balance that can benefit your emotional well-being and your overall health." There are many forms and styles of meditation, and finding one that works for you can make all the difference in handling stress.

Others practice yoga. The various poses, breathing techniques, and mental relaxation involved help practitioners melt away the pressures of daily life. As discussed in a previous chapter, yoga is good not only for your body but also excellent for your mind. It helps you find what centers you and brings inner peace.

Some people enjoy going for a walk, breathing fresh air, and connecting with nature. There's something about being outdoors that helps the mind. Natural sunlight, sounds, and smells bring us back to nature and can help ease stress or provide a way to cope with it.[14] This includes exercising outdoors. If the weather is nice, get off the treadmill and walk or run outside. Swim for cardiovascular health, or be bold and do all your exercises outside.

Others turn to hobbies, writing, or simply "unplugging" for a while. The key is not to escape to avoid your problems but to escape to refresh yourself. Avoidance only adds to the stress. Instead, recharge, remain calm, and figure out how to tackle what's stressing you. It can help you write down what's worrying you and come up with a plan for how to address or cope with each concern. Seeing things on paper and working through them can be an excellent way to achieve your goals. No matter how you handle stress, to stay fit and healthy over 50, you must manage it and not let it consume you.

---

[14] White, M.P., Alcock, I., Grellier, J. et al. Spending at least 120 minutes a week in nature is associated with good health and wellbeing. Sci Rep 9, 7730 (2019).

Caloric Deficit

We've mentioned the phrase "caloric deficit" several times, but what does it mean? In its simplest terms, the goal of losing weight depends on burning more calories per day than you consume. By combining exercise and regular activity, you burn calories; the key is to ingest fewer calories than you expend. This deficit will enable you to lose weight. Your body will then need to tap into its natural energy reserves—your fat cells—to produce more energy. This is why fitness trackers that count your steps are so popular. Awareness of your movement helps you understand if you are burning enough calories. A calorie is a unit of energy defined by the heat needed to raise the temperature of water by one degree. Knowing the scientific definition of a calorie isn't important, but knowing how much you ingest through food and drink and how much you burn is crucial.

As discussed in earlier chapters about carbohydrates, specifically the good and bad sugars, a sugary cola drink can contain as much as 39 grams of sugar. There are about four calories in a gram of sugar, so a single can of soda contains roughly 156 calories. Remember, you can't out-exercise a bad diet. To lose weight, you must make real choices about what you consume. If you consume fewer calories but don't exercise, your body could slow down its metabolism and expend less energy. Although diet is paramount, you need to move your body to create the demand for more energy.

On the flip side, if your goal is to gain weight—specifically muscle mass—you need to follow a different dietary strategy. For example, if you want to build muscle, you need to increase your protein intake so that your calories come from protein. Exercise causes muscles to tear and repair (on a micro level), as discussed earlier. To repair and build muscle, your body needs amino acids, which are the building blocks of protein. Getting your calories from protein allows your body to repair itself more effectively.

As emphasized throughout this book, a balanced exercise program and a good diet have incredible benefits. To achieve your fitness goals, it's essential to understand your diet, caloric intake, and the primary sources of your calories. Planning, writing things down, and knowing your numbers, reps, and intake will remove the guesswork from being fit over 50.

Cold—Hot?

One of the latest fitness crazes is cold water plunges or baths. This may not be as wild as it sounds. Cold plunges provide a short burst of cortisol, which can help moderate overall stress levels. [15,16] Ice baths may also boost your mood, alleviate anxiety and depression, and help maintain testosterone levels. This might be something you've never thought of trying, but it could be the missing ingredient to managing your testosterone levels and stress.

You must follow some important guidelines while participating in cold water plunges. Make sure to breathe calmly and steadily, allowing you to control your mind and emotions. It's recommended to do a cold water plunge early in the day as it can boost your energy levels, which you don't want to interfere with your sleep patterns. The typical water temperature for a plunge is between 50–60 degrees Fahrenheit. If you prefer a colder temperature, gradually work your way down. If you plunge outdoors during the winter, the water may be even colder. It's also beneficial to let your body reheat naturally.

Although cold water plunges are now used for metabolic health, they've long been used by athletes. Many

---

[15] Srámek P, Simecková M, Janský L, Savlíková J, Vybíral S. Human physiological responses to immersion into water of different temperatures. Eur J Appl Physiol. 2000 Mar;81(5):436-42. doi: 10.1007/s004210050065. PMID: 10751106.

[16] Mooventhan A, Nivethitha L. Scientific evidence-based effects of hydrotherapy on various systems of the body. N Am J Med Sci. 2014 May;6(5):199-209. doi: 10.4103/1947-2714.132935. PMID: 24926444; PMCID: PMC4049052.

college and professional athletic programs provide "cold tubs" for players to use after games or practices as part of their recovery.

Cold plunges have been shown to help regulate cortisol levels, which are responsible for the fight-or-flight response. Lowering overall cortisol levels helps reduce stress-related tension. In fact, from the first time someone steps into cold water, the fight-or-flight reflex is triggered. Do you face an uncomfortable environment (fight), or do you walk away (flight)? There are many benefits, and further research is ongoing. Cold water plunges were initially used to soothe sore muscles, reduce inflammation, and lower core body temperature. Today, the overall health benefits of cold water are gaining more recognition.[17]

What about heat? Saunas are making a comeback due to their natural ability to restore and maintain health. They provide relaxation while reducing stress. Saunas are also excellent for pain relief, as they relax muscles and reduce inflammation. The cardiovascular benefits of using a sauna

---

[17] Esperland D, de Weerd L, Mercer JB. Health effects of voluntary exposure to cold water - a continuing subject of debate. Int J Circumpolar Health. 2022 Dec;81(1):2111789. doi: 10.1080/22423982.2022.2111789. PMID: 36137565; PMCID: PMC9518606.

are comparable to those of short, effective workouts.[18] A session will elevate your heart rate and blood pressure, similar to exercise.

For those new to saunas, it's advisable to start with 5–10 minutes per day. As you become more accustomed, you can extend the session to 20 minutes per day, and experienced users can go up to 30 minutes. It's also important to stay hydrated, as saunas cause significant sweating.

If you combine an ice plunge with a sauna, experts recommend going from hot to cold. As mentioned earlier, letting your body warm up naturally after an ice plunge is a good idea. The combination of heat and ice is increasingly popular in wellness treatments, as it promotes natural healing while helping you manage external stressors and their effects on your hormones.

Limitation of Matter

I saved this topic for the end. "Limitation of Matter" is an old chiropractic term, a self-explanatory phrase. This concept applies to physical or mental limitations, such as a

---

[18] S. Ketelhut, R.G. Ketelhut. The blood pressure and heart rate during sauna bath correspond to cardiac responses during submaximal dynamic exercise. Complementary Therapies in Medicine, 2019; 44: 218

lost limb, organ damage, or mental health challenges. These are real issues that can limit one's ability to reach full fitness potential. It can also refer to chronic illnesses, whether congenital or developed later in life. This book never diminishes the reality that genuine physical, mental, or emotional limitations can prevent someone from achieving all they aspire to. Let me tell you about Kyle Landi, a bodybuilder born with Down Syndrome. Kyle has inspired many and has a very active social media presence. He also competed in the 2023 Arnold Schwarzenegger Classic. Despite the challenges he faces, ambition and motivation are not limited. Another example is Jim Abbott, who was born with one hand. Jim played baseball for the University of Michigan, won the James E. Sullivan Award for the nation's best amateur athlete, and pitched a no-hitter with the New York Yankees. Earlier in this book, I spoke about an individual named Jim who lives with paraplegia. He would exercise with the rest of us in the gym and hold everyone accountable.

Even with a "limitation of matter," you can still eat right, take vitamins, and exercise at your own pace and level. Breathing and sweating are not reserved for only certain people. Anyone can set their own goals and work toward them. As mentioned earlier in this book, don't live in someone else's world—focus on your world and set your goals to be as fit and healthy as possible.

There are many documented benefits to focusing on fitness. Exercise is good for mental health and self-esteem. Clean food, supplements, and antioxidants are accessible to everyone. No matter how bad your day is or how off you may feel, get up, go to the gym, and start with just one exercise. Get your body moving, whether it's a stretch, a light walk, or something more intense.

These suggestions are not just ideas but important elements you should incorporate into your journey to staying fit over 50. We live in a society where obesity and medication overuse are common. Don't settle for average; we only go through this world once—push yourself physically and mentally. At the start of this book, we talked about Jack LaLanne, Chuck Norris, and Joan Campbell. These are just three of the many people who have fought or are still fighting the effects of aging and refuse to surrender. Pick up a biography of someone fit over 50 and see how they did it. Plenty of social media influencers work on their fitness; follow them and study their thought processes—you'll often find that it's a mindset. If you're just beginning, no matter your age, start today. Start simple and then work your way up the ladder of health and fitness. If others can do it, so can you. If others can stay fit, recover from a "cheat day," and not give up after setbacks, we can all learn from them. This book was written because I want to see people fit, off medication, and living longer, healthier lives. I'm rooting for you. Are you rooting for yourself? All it takes is to stand up for your health and fitness. Be healthy, be fit, and stay young!

Chapter Eleven: Let's Get Started

You've read this book, highlighted important parts, left notes in the margins, and reread sections that resonate with you. Now, what's next? First, stay calm. This is a lot of information to take in, but it can help you become and stay fit through your 50s, 60s, 70s, and beyond. No matter your age or what you have or haven't achieved in the past, you can always work toward being better, stronger, and fitter.

I like to write things down to make them clear and visible. You can jot down your goals on your phone, computer, or even a yellow legal pad, but the key is to start listing them. I always recommend working backward. Begin with your final objective (goal) and work backward from there. Page 1: What is your ultimate goal? Know that when you reach this goal, it's time to set a new one. Stagnation and complacency lead to decline; each goal is just another rung on the ladder of life.

Once you have your goal, think about what you need to do to achieve it. Create columns for exercise, nutrition, supplements, and incidentals—each column representing something essential to reaching your goal. Then, under each column, list the exercises you plan to do, the dietary changes you want to make, the supplements you want to add, and so on. Break it down even further: exactly which exercises, how many reps, how much weight, which foods, what portions, and what you need to purchase. This will create a detailed plan to help you achieve success. As you progress, you may need to make adjustments, add new goals, or pivot depending on your progress, but this plan will provide a clear path to follow.

I also recommend taking ideas from this book and writing them into your notebook to stay focused. It's natural to have low points and days with low energy. Some days, you'll need a good kick in the butt to get moving, but positive quotes, sayings, and ideas can help keep you excited and focused on reaching your ultimate goal.

I suggest harnessing your positive energy when you feel motivated. Write down how you're feeling, what you plan to do, how you'll do it, and why you're motivated. Capture those emotions, thoughts, and physical reactions. Then, on days when you're lacking energy, revisit your own words to reignite that spark. Napoleon Hill, in Think and Grow Rich, spoke about reading your own words every day, first thing in the morning and right before bed. This helps plant positive thoughts in your mind at the start and end of each day.

No one said getting fit would be easy—it's a process. Find joy in the process. Celebrate your small accomplishments, then refocus on your next goal. If you fall off track—whether it's your eating plan or missing workouts—don't get discouraged. We're all human. Just get back to your notebook, see where you left off, and pick up from there. You're not racing anyone; you're working toward your fitness. Consistency and accountability will lead you to success.

Enjoy your time at the gym; don't see it as a chore but as a daily challenge. Choose foods you enjoy, regardless of your eating style, and simply modify how you eat them. There are plenty of food options within each dietary approach, so find what works for you. Keep learning—this book is meant to introduce and motivate you to become and stay fit for life. There are countless other books, videos, and articles on the specific topics discussed here. Dive deeper into the aspects that interest you. This book provides an overview, guiding you toward fitness, but you can delve further into particular diets, exercise styles, or supplements. Things are always advancing—stay up-to-date with the latest research. Ten years ago, if someone suggested cold plunges for health, you might have thought they were crazy, but today, it's a common practice and is becoming even more popular. The same goes for eating keto or the importance of stretching. Stay open to new developments and technologies that can help you achieve your goals. Continuous learning benefits both your brain and overall fitness.

Life is a journey, and so is fitness. Enjoy the ride. It may get bumpy at times, but when you were a child and fell off your bike, you dusted yourself off and got back on. Don't let minor setbacks stop you. Life is too short. Staying fit will add years to your life and life to your years. Now, go out there and stay fit over 50, 60, 70, and beyond!

Printed in Great Britain
by Amazon

62594930R00131